TRAVELTAGE

Use Your Smartphone and the Fulfillment by Amazon Program to Make Money, Travel, and Create the Life You Want!

Cover Images obtained from Istockphoto.com.

Written by Timothy Hess

Published by Supine Lupine Press, LLC

Edited by Janie Johns

Paperback ISBN: 978-0-9903795-0-8

www.Traveltage.com

CONTENTS

ACKNOWLEDGEMENTS

I am grateful to the following people whose invaluable wisdom and guidance has helped me write this book and achieve success in this business:

Steve Weber, author of *Barcode Booty: How I found and sold $2 million of 'junk' on eBay and Amazon, And you can, too, using your phone*, and many books too numerous to mention.
http://www.weberbooks.com

Chris Green, CEO of ScanPower and author of *Arbitrage: The authoritative guide on how it works, why it works, and how it can work for you* (Formerly *Retail Arbitrage*)
http://www.ScanPower.com

Cynthia Stine, author of *Make Thousands on Amazon in 10 Hours a Week! How I Turned $200 Into $40,000+ Gross Sales My First Year in Part-Time Online Sales!*
http://www.fbastepbystep.com

Nathan Holmquist, author of *Selling on Amazon's FBA Program - Earn $2-5K Per Month Shipping Boxes of Books to Amazon*
http://www.booktothefuture.com

Janie Johns, Editor Extraordinaire

Additional Contributors:

Dave & Jeannice Perry

Leisha Bevoni

Sascha

FOREWORD

For decades, I've been fascinated with selling things via the Internet. Back in the pre-Internet days, the big challenge was finding customers, which usually required some type of advertising. If you weren't careful, you'd spend too much on advertising, and not have any profit left over.

The home-based niche business came of age with the advent of the Internet. Selling via the Web, you could let your customers find you instead of wasting your time and money searching for them. When eBay and Amazon achieved critical mass back in the 1990s, a whole new generation of Internet entrepreneurs was born. With virtually no startup costs, the opportunity was wide open for anyone who wanted to start their own business selling used, reconditioned, closeout, or collectible items.

The biggest challenge about doing business online is that conditions change rapidly. Internet entrepreneurs must stay nimble and adapt to changing circumstances, or their business will suffer.

The good news is that changing conditions always bring new opportunities. When I first got into online selling, Half.com was the king of the hill. eBay wasn't far behind, and Amazon was just beginning to dabble in third-party selling. To put it mildly, things have changed.

A variety of changes over the past few years have turned Amazon's third-party selling platform and its Fulfillment by Amazon (FBA) program into an attractive opportunity for sellers who want to sell virtually anything – new and used merchandise, or even niche items you'd find at the corner store. Many folks have grumbled about these changes, but many others have seized the opportunity. And the opportunity is so vast that it's possible for anyone with a moderate level of organizational skill to start a new business from scratch. That's exactly the kind of opportunity Tim Hess explains in Traveltage. Tim shows you how you can travel while simultaneously running your business.

Virtually anyone can take his example and run with it, or adapt it to their own personal style.

One thing that hasn't changed about online selling and entrepreneurship in general – it's a fascinating, fulfilling pursuit unlike any other. For those of us who've discovered it, it hardly feels like work at all. Instead, it's a lucrative, entertaining, challenge that you won't find in any 9 to 5 job.

Is it a get-rich-quick scheme? Of course not. And it's not easy. It requires dedication to every transaction, an obsession with details to try to keep things from going wrong. And when things do go wrong, you've got to have the ability to let it go, and to not worry about the things that aren't under your control (which are many).

Just as it's always been, online selling is part art, part science. Nowadays, thanks to wireless price-checking, you can check prices and forecast your profits with a good degree of accuracy. But there is no substitute for experience – the lessons learned you'll acquire from your first year or two in business.

Read this book and the good advice you'll find here. Realize that opportunity is all around you, and that you really can enjoy traveling and running a profitable business using Tim's "Traveltage" techniques. You've got quite an adventure ahead of you. Dive in!

—Steve Weber

WHAT'S IN A NAME?

Traveltage! The word conjures up visions of...nothing! Webster defines Traveltage as, well, Webster doesn't define it at all, because it's a word I coined to describe my spin on the practice of traveling combined with Retail Arbitrage (buying products from retail sources and profiting from their resale).

Retail Arbitrage is the term popularized by author Chris Green. Combining Retail Arbitrage, with travel is a perfect combination:

Travel + Arbitrage = Traveltage

Technically, it would be "Traveltrage," but that's tougher to say, so Traveltage it is!

After reading Steve Weber's *Barcode Booty* (http://amzn.to/1goIhxw) and Chris Green's *Retail Arbitrage* (http://amzn.to/1oZfdiQ) I immediately took action (that very afternoon) and was astounded by the results I got. I found these books when I was seeking to supplement the dwindling income from my job.

With my background dabbling in real estate, stocks, and precious metals, I am well-versed in traditional investments. But nothing in my investing experience has come close to the return on investment I'm routinely making from Retail Arbitrage coupled with Fulfillment by Amazon (FBA). I'm also having an absolute blast doing it, which I cannot truthfully say about my other investments (tenants, maintenance, and market fluctuations are no fun).

The FBA service and the art of Traveltage allows me to travel and be a "solopreneur" (one person entrepreneur), running my business anywhere I can get cell phone reception and find products to sell. Throughout this book, I will describe exactly how I do it, and how you can, too.

Have you always dreamed of working for yourself, but haven't known how to go about it? Has the prospect of being an entrepreneur left you paralyzed with too many choices, concerns and fears? Have you wanted to travel, but found the costs prohibitive?

What if you could work for yourself *while* traveling, simultaneously making money and outsourcing many of the day-to-day headaches of business that have kept you from staking your claim as an entrepreneur? YOU CAN!

I hope the ideas in this book inspire you to think without limitation. I really push the envelope of what's possible because I like to challenge myself and reach new vistas. Sometimes that means I inadvertently create more stress and complication in my life. I'm OK with that because I hate to stagnate, and I have a high tolerance for discomfort. My life's not always rosy, but I see this as the price to pay for personal growth. Keep these thoughts in mind as you implement the strategies I describe.

If you have any thoughts on what to include in a future edition, want to share your successes, or just want to say hi, email me at: Tim@Traveltage.com.

CHAPTER 1

THE TRAVELTAGE CONCEPT

Before learning of the amazing opportunities of Traveltage, I was a seasoned traveler, with a lot of domestic and international travel experience for both work and leisure. I look back with fond memories on my travels, but it's a little bittersweet – after all, I probably could have paid for my trips, or at least paid for a significant portion of them, by sourcing high margin items, and having a great time doing it! Not to mention, the incredible return on my investment of time and money would have allowed me a better lifestyle and a quicker route to independence from a traditional "day job." Nonetheless, I have no regrets, and I'm happy that these opportunities have come my way.

The FBA program was introduced in 2008 and most of the scouting apps and ancillary products are likewise only a few years old. This is in many respects still a ground-floor opportunity.

The technology making all this possible has evolved to a point where it's now practical to get real-time data to make important buying decisions rapidly, decisively, and profitably, all in the palm of your hand. Furthermore, it's now such a wireless world that you can run this business anywhere you choose. Say goodbye to your boss and the constraints that have kept you tethered to any particular location.

WHAT'S NOT IN THIS BOOK

Because there are many authors who have already contributed to this body of knowledge, I have chosen to avoid repeating their work. This book therefore will be of the most value to people already familiar with the process of sourcing, shipping, and selling products via the Fulfillment by Amazon service.

I will not be covering basic topics such as how to list inventory, how to contact Amazon customer support, how to navigate the Amazon shipping process flow, how to deal with negative feedback, or anything of this nature. These fundamental topics, while crucial to any seller's success, have been duly covered by those who have come before me, and you can find more information about their books in the Recommended Reading section of this book.

If you're new to Traveltage, you can shorten your learning curve by reading the books and referencing the other information sources I recommend. I also recommend that you refer to the Amazon help files and forums. There is a wealth of information available in those files, and they will help you with mastering the basics.

Here are some useful links to get you started:

Amazon Seller Resources (http://amzn.to/1kv32Gw)

Amazon Seller Forums (http://bit.ly/1iKyGQM)

Amazon Seller Support Blog (http://bit.ly/R1AIRO)

Fulfillment by Amazon (http://bit.ly/1n4uv2I)

Selling on Amazon (http://amzn.to/1hYq6ck)

Selling on Amazon FAQs (http://amzn.to/1oZg2YV)

While this may seem overwhelming, rest assured that the principles of this business are really very simple.

In a nutshell:

1. Use your smartphone to scout for items that you can sell at a profit.

2. List your items on Amazon.com.

3. Ship your items to an FBA warehouse.

4. Generate sales.

5. Get paid.

FOR INTERNATIONAL READERS

This book is admittedly United States centric. I can't help that, since I'm a U.S. citizen, and my experience with these techniques has heretofore been confined to the U.S. I intend to provide additional information for worldwide opportunities in the future. Please visit my blog at www.Traveltage.com, and join my mailing list. If the situation warrants, and if there is enough demand, I will write another book encompassing global opportunities.

If you purchased this book for international Traveltage information, you will still find it valuable, and will be able to modify the information to suit your particular circumstances. You should be able to implement the same strategies I outline, wherever you find yourself in the world. It's all about creativity and flexibility. These attributes are more important to your success than anything else.

You may be able to ship items from your particular location to an Amazon warehouse in the U.S. (although the logistics and costs of shipping may make this prohibitive), or to one of the many fulfillment centers that Amazon is increasingly opening worldwide. As of this writing, Amazon has fulfillment centers in the UK, Germany, France, Italy, China, Japan, and Canada.

To learn more or register for an account:

FBA International (http://amzn.to/1mcVNE3)

PAYING THE TAX MAN

I know it's cliché, but what's that quote about death and taxes? Yup, they're the only things in life that are certain! Sure, they're unavoidable, but why not have a strategy to minimize your taxes and maximize your profits? The topic has been covered *ad nauseam* elsewhere, and I'm no tax expert, but I would like to call your attention to some information that you may not have considered.

CAUTION!: Before attempting this, obtain advice for your personal situation from a competent tax professional, or the IRS themselves. You can contact the IRS at: taxforms@irs.gov.

Did you know that as a U.S. citizen, you can legally pay no taxes on the first $92,000 you earn, as long as you spend 11 months of the year outside the U.S.? Traveling for 11 months of the year (all the while sourcing new merchandise for your business), and then coming back for a month sounds like a pretty nice lifestyle! If you have a spouse, he/she can do the same. That means between the two of you, your first $184,000 earned annually is legally tax free. Not bad – pretty sure you can live on it!

You could also choose to come back a few days/weeks at a time, to source products for your business domestically, visit family and friends, and make sure your housekeeper/property manager is doing their job!

You'll need to track your time in and out of the country carefully. The IRS verifies your presence outside the country with the "Bona Fide Residence" and "Physical Presence" tests. If you're interested in pursuing this, here are some IRS resources to review:

> Form 2555: Foreign Earned Income (http://1.usa.gov/SqLFgt)
>
> Publication 54: Tax Guide for U.S. Citizens and Resident Aliens Abroad (http://1.usa.gov/1k0I3rm)

Maybe you're saying "But I can't just up and leave! I've got a family, a business, a house, (insert other obligation here)." My goal is to present you with options that may not have occurred to you. I understand that not everyone has the luxury, flexibility, or even the desire to gallivant around the world. However, as a business person, you probably wouldn't mind paying less taxes, whether you're traveling, or staying put. The money you save in taxes can be put to use to grow your business faster.

The high margins from Traveltage create mind-boggling rates of return. If you're a proficient scout, using a good scouting application, you should have no trouble regularly achieving 100-300% profits. This figure is not annually, this is often **WEEKLY** or **MONTHLY**, depending on the merchandise you choose and how quickly it sells.

You will find that you can make even more than 100-300% on many occasions. Generally speaking, you will make these types of returns on items that you buy for perhaps one dollar, and sell for $5, $10, $20, or more.

These margins represent a huge return on your investment, but you will need to sell significant volume to make appreciable income. Fortunately, there are opportunities virtually everywhere.

Most investment formulas are based on **ANNUAL** returns, and it's frequently considered extraordinary to achieve 20% annually. Check out any financial magazine, or popular investment book. Note how they are crowing about 20% annual returns. Below are figures for a 100% return, compounded monthly. How does this compare to your current investments in stocks, options, bonds, real estate, Forex, or precious metals?

Inputs		
Current Principal:	$	10,000.00
Annual Addition:	$	0.00
Years to grow:		1
Interest Rate:		100 %
Compound interest	12	time(s) annually
Make additions at ◉ start ○ end of each compounding period		
	Calculate	
Results		
Future Value:	$	26,130.35

$10,000 X 100% Return Compounded Monthly
Source: Moneychimp.com

If making $26,000 from a $10,000 investment doesn't excite you, what would? What about beating every known investment with minimal risk, maximum control, and boatloads of freedom, isn't exciting? What's more, how much control do you have over traditional investments? With all of them, you are at the mercy of the market! A scandal with a company (think Enron, WorldCom, Lehman Brothers, etc.), and the stock you own plummets. Or, the general economy suffers (kinda like what's happening today) and your real estate value plummets. Precious metals? Yes, they make sense, primarily as a hedge against inflation, but check out the following charts:

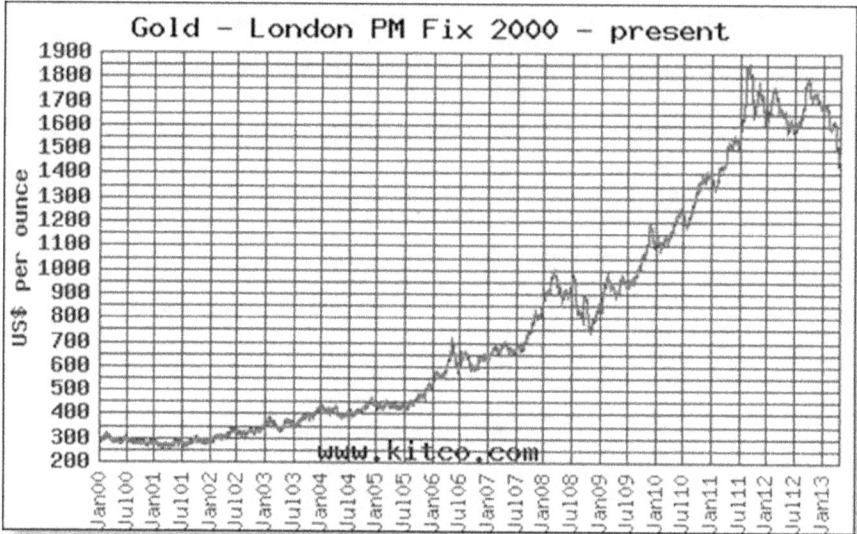

Gold 13 Year Return

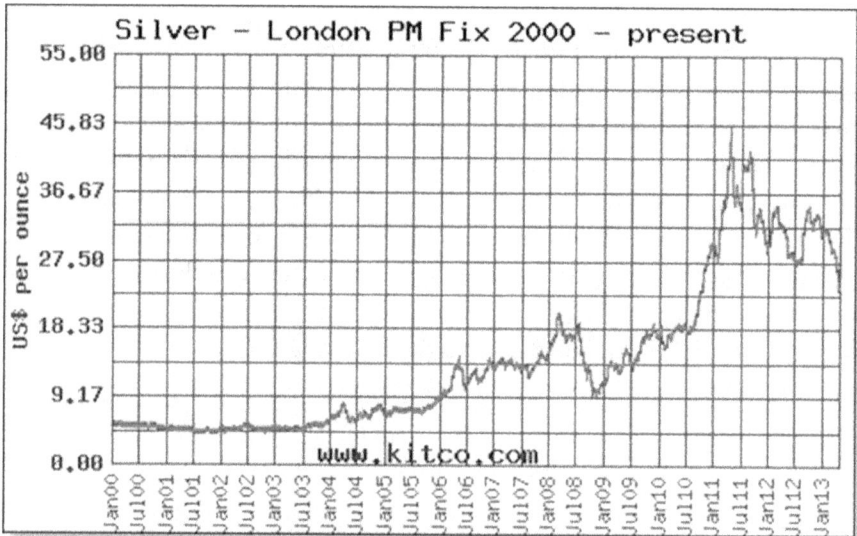

Silver 13 Year Return
Source: Kitco.com

Impressive results, for sure, BUT, this was a return over thirteen years! And look at the volatility, not to mention how long you had to wait to get the return. With arbitrage, you're frequently getting these returns weekly, monthly, or at the very least annually. And, your risk is mitigated by holding as many products as you can source. It's the whole "don't put your eggs in one basket" theory exemplified.

Would you rather hold a portfolio of 10 stocks, each with $1,000 invested, or take the same $10,000 and invest it in hundreds or thousands of individual products, each with a high margin and low downside risk? Not to mention, which is easier – going to a retail store like Walgreens and finding low-price, high-margin items, or sifting through stocks and evaluating all the market factors to determine if they are a good investment? Score one point for Walgreens.

Deodorant, shampoo, cosmetics, nutritional supplements, toys and knick-knacks will always have a market. More people buy these items than stocks. These are evergreen commodities that always have demand. Furthermore, when you invest in stocks, real estate, precious metals, Forex, etc., your mistakes, or major market moves against you, can be devastating. This simply isn't an issue with Traveltage unless you buy bulk products (such as ordering products from a wholesaler) which turn out to be duds. If you do decide to order from a wholesaler, you can mitigate much of the risk by first testing the market with a minimum order.

Naturally, once you have mastered the techniques of Traveltage on a small scale, you will want to consider growing your business with larger quantities of inventory. You will need to locate sources of replenishable inventory (since clearance items – the primary source of Retail Arbitrage inventory, are limited in quantity/availability). Wholesale channels are a common way to reach more sales volume.

But all in good time. There is a natural progression to learn this business and avoid costly errors. Begin with Retail Arbitrage since you can start very small, minimizing errors, and rapidly sharpening your business acumen. Once you're more seasoned, you can commit to larger inventory buys (perhaps via wholesale channels).

On occasion you will choose products that are duds, but if you are mainly sourcing clearance "onesie" and "twosie" items, you will only be able to purchase a limited supply (because there's a limited amount available in the store). This automatically insulates you against over-investing in a potential non-seller. You can always lower your price and accept a lower margin, in the event sales lag. The product will probably sell, albeit sometimes for less than you hoped, but it won't go to zero (which is a distinct possibility with other investments). Worst case, you can have the item shipped back to you to sell through another channel, such as eBay.

A great advantage of Retail Arbitrage is that you can invest tiny amounts of money and build a significant business. I use $10,000 as an example, but you can use any amount at your disposal. You can even begin for free by sourcing products like books, DVDs, or other items you already own. Free books are often available from friends or family who simply don't want them anymore. How do you think all those books end up at thrift stores? Or, you can find them at community centers, where people donate them when they're done with them.

If you source from thrift stores, garage sales, drug stores, etc., it's not uncommon to find items for fifty cents to a dollar that will sell for $10, $20, or more. For example, board games gathering dust, sitting on shelves at thrift stores, can be had for one or two dollars, and will often sell for $40 or more. This is a 2,000% return for a $2 board game. Can you do that routinely, easily, and with virtually no risk, with any other investment? If so, let's do lunch – I'm buying!

I know this may sound too good to be true. There are naysayers who will shout "impossible!" or "those are isolated instances" and other invectives, and accuse me of sensationalizing my results, but I assure you it's possible, even probable, if you get out there and follow these proven principles. Sure, there is risk – the amount you pay for the item, and the nominal shipping/storage fees at Amazon's FBA warehouses. Are you willing to risk $2 to make $40? How much did you spend on your education? On lunch? Your house? Are you getting this type of return on investment from those?

Even if you don't believe that these types of deals are possible (though, they are actually not difficult to find), you can do just fine scouting deals in retail stores, never setting foot in a thrift store or pawing through used items at a garage sale.

In most retail stores, there is plenty of clearance merchandise available. Most of it has been marked down multiple times and has had no takers. As a general rule, I like to focus around the $10-$20 range, and aim for a 300% mark up. After the fees that Amazon charges are deducted, as well as acquisition and inbound shipping costs, following this guideline results in a 100% return on my investment.

I will occasionally stray from these criteria when the situation warrants. If I can purchase an item for $50 and sell it for $200, it's worth bending the rules. Likewise, if an item has a very favorable sales rank, like 100, but will return 30%, I'm in. With such a low sales rank, it's virtually certain that the item will sell quickly, and I'm happy to scoop up a 30% return in just a few days. (Wall Street, eat your heart out!)

I would rather purchase 10 items at $10 each, than one item at $100. This allows me to spread risk because the chances of those 10 items selling are better than a single high dollar item selling. Plus, despite my best efforts, inevitably, some of my items get returned by customers and are not resalable. In this event, a $10 loss is less painful than $100.

THIS SOUNDS TOO GOOD TO BE TRUE

I distrust authors who use hyperbole, so I'll attempt to refrain from doing so.

I have deliberately used conservative examples for the sake of illustrating the types of returns you can achieve in this business. You can routinely make a much higher return on your investment; it's not uncommon to make 300-1,000%. It's all a matter of the items you choose to sell, your cost to acquire them, and the going rate of the items in the marketplace at any given time.

Granted, you will not make this amount on ALL of the items you sell on Amazon; sometimes you'll make much more, and sometimes you'll break even or take a loss, despite your best efforts. No one bats a thousand all the time, not even huge retailers like Walmart, who frequently must discount merchandise because it couldn't be sold at a higher retail price. Incidentally, this is the very *reason* that opportunity for buying low and selling on Amazon is a viable possibility for savvy solopreneurs.

The marketplace is constantly in flux, and you will find that your sales will wax and wane accordingly. A seasonal item such as a Christmas toy may sell at a premium close to Christmas but garner little to no interest at other times of the year. Those Valentine's Day gifts on February 16th, or the Halloween-themed items on November 1st, always sell at a steep discount, but will have some demand year-round (and definitely when the season comes around again).

One lucrative strategy is to buy seasonal or holiday items which are always discounted after the season or holiday passes and then hold them until they are in vogue again. With Traveltage, however, this may not always be practical. As always, you'll need to evaluate whether the margin and logistics of the situation warrant the purchase, on a case by case basis. If the item meets your criteria, and you can't pass it up (but you don't want to pay FBA storage fees out of season), consider sending one or two to FBA to act as "long tail" items (defined as items that have low sales volume) which may sell, albeit after an extended period of time, and then ship the remaining inventory to your home or to a friend's for safekeeping, until you return from your travels. For more information on long tail items, see the book *The Long Tail* (http://amzn.to/1goJ7dL), by Chris Anderson. I will only consider a long tail item if the margin is significant enough to warrant the inevitable long-term holding period while waiting for it to sell. My preference is to choose fast-selling inventory to minimize storage fees and reinvest my profits, rapidly growing my business.

CHAPTER 2

THE NUTS AND BOLTS OF TRAVELTAGE

I won't tell you that Traveltage is easy. But, it's not exactly difficult either. Expect to encounter some challenges. But throughout your journey, you will sharpen your skills, and after you have a few successes under your belt, new challenges will be less daunting.

I find that I'm most creative when I need to be. There is also a triumph of the spirit that comes from overcoming obstacles. It's very satisfying.

TRIAL RUN

One of the best ways to gain confidence is with a trial run, when you're not traveling at all. Start small and ramp up as your confidence grows. Assemble all the essentials you plan to use on your travels, and then take them on a dry run to test your methods. Can you go to a local store, bring the items to your car, pack them in the parking lot, go to the library, print your labels, and then drop them off at a shipping location such as Staples, Office Depot, or a UPS Store? Congrats! That's all there is to it in any other location, too!

I have successfully sourced items in various cities in the U.S. from coast to coast. You can do the same. When you do find yourself in a new location, start small. Source just a few items that will ship in one or two boxes. Once you have faith that you can do this anywhere, the sky's the limit.

One of these days, I plan to go on a "Traveltage National Parks Road Trip" traveling to all the beautiful national parks across the U.S., snapping up every bargain I can find along the way. I don't see any reason why I can't deduct the trip, have a blast, and travel to my heart's content. Sure beats a cubicle!

When I first tried Traveltage, I was successful, but it was a much more stressful experience than it needed to be. I was in Santa Monica, CA, for the first time, and I was just beginning to see the beauty and power of leveraging Amazon FBA with Retail Arbitrage. My mind was not only buzzing with all kinds of possibilities for augmenting my FBA inventory, but also with fear that I couldn't pull this off. Here are some of the many questions that were weighing me down:

- What if I can't find a place to ship my merchandise?
- Where do I get boxes?
- How do I weigh my items?
- How do I print labels, packing slips, etc.?
- Where do I stage items for shipping?
- What do I use for packing material?
- What time does my flight leave, and do I have enough time to pack and ship?
- Did I leave the stove on, back home?

I needed answers!

First, I went down to the beach and took a deep breath. Second, I realized that this can be done anywhere, because there are retailers, shippers, and opportunities everywhere. In essence, everything is the same as what you do at home, except the location! Granted, you need to be resourceful, but you will soon find it is straightforward and can be done traveling, in a very similar fashion, to when you're at home.

If you have not already done so, I recommend that you read Steve Weber's *Barcode Booty* (http://amzn.to/1goIhxw), and Chris Green's *Arbitrage* (http://amzn.to/1oZfdiQ). These books will lay the foundation of the process for you. Then apply the principles I outline here, and you'll see the world of opportunity all around you.

I don't recommend attempting Traveltage until you've mastered the basics. The fact is, you will make mistakes, and there is a learning curve. Traveltage adds additional variables such as time constraints, foreign environments, and various distractions/stressors that aren't issues back home. So, if you're completely new, don't do this until you have the basics mastered. Now, let's address the questions:

WHAT IF I CAN'T FIND A PLACE TO SHIP MY MERCHANDISE?

This turned out to be a ridiculous, unwarranted fear. If you're anywhere near civilization, there will be shipping options. Staples and Office Depot ship via UPS, and they will accept your packages for free when you prepay through your Amazon account.

You can also download the UPS app on your smartphone, and have access to all nearby shipping locations. Or, you can call 1-800-PICKUPS to have UPS pick up your boxes on location. There is a fee for this (typically $10 or less), and you will need to have a UPS account (available free at www.UPS.com).

Depending on where you are staying, there may already be a scheduled pickup, allowing you to add your boxes at no additional charge. This is an elegant, simple, and effective solution. You can prepare your shipments in your hotel room, and then leave them at the front desk.

WHERE DO I GET BOXES?

Yet another unwarranted fear. Boxes are so ubiquitous that it's a non-issue. Just about every product is shipped in boxes, so there's no shortage!

Is there a restaurant, grocery store, discount store, drug store, office supply store, or other retail store nearby? If you ask politely, you will find as many boxes as you need. You may need to go to more than one source, but you're practicing Traveltage, so you're doing that anyway, right?

If you're in a grocery store and the deli doesn't have any boxes, then try the floral department, or produce, or dairy. If you strike out, ask where else you might find them. Harbor Freight Tools often has boxes free for the taking, and they get shipments almost daily. Ditto for Walmart.

You will often find boxes behind strip malls, in alleys, and various other places. I've also had success asking managers/employees for boxes while I have a full shopping cart or two in tow. Something on the order of the following should do the trick:

> "Wow! I didn't anticipate finding so many bargains! They don't sell 'em like this back home. Since I'm traveling, I'm gonna need to ship this stuff. You wouldn't have any boxes, would you?"

I find that most people's paradigm is completely blown when I roll up with shopping carts overflowing with merchandise. When they get over the shock, they will often treat me like a V.I.P., since I'm about to drop a huge wad of cash at their store and relieve them of the headaches of this inventory that they want to move. This tends to make them accommodating with little graces like free boxes. Plus, I really am doing them a favor – freeing precious retail space for more profitable items. Everyone wins!

Finally, if you've been flitting about the city scooping up bargains (which is the point, right?), and you simply cannot find free boxes (unlikely), you can purchase boxes at office supply stores or UPS stores (the same ones you'll be shipping from). This will cut into your margin, but if you don't have enough margin to absorb the cost of a box here and there, you probably don't have enough margin to sell the items profitably via FBA in the first place.

You don't necessarily need to confine your shipping choices to UPS. Obviously, Fed-Ex, USPS, and others are viable options – you just won't benefit from the steep discounts that Amazon has negotiated with UPS. Also, using UPS is advantageous because the Amazon process flow is streamlined for it, and Amazon reimburses shipping damages with minimal effort.

HOW DO I WEIGH MY ITEMS?

Did I mention irrational fears? There are a few solutions to this:

Solution 1:

Get the weight from the product listing on Amazon. Admittedly, this has some inherent pitfalls. The item may not be listed on Amazon at all, so you would not have access to any weight information. Or, the item may be incorrectly listed, resulting in an inaccurate weight. Still, it's better than nothing.

Solution 2:

Weigh the item using a portable shipping scale, or digital luggage scale. I like to travel as light as possible, following a "less is more" approach. My preference is to use a digital luggage scale, which weighs just a few ounces and is very compact. I use the AWS LS-110 (http://amzn.to/1jczvgN), available on Amazon for about $15. It is very accurate and simple to use. I also use the

AWS PS-25 digital postal scale (http://amzn.to/1niRmLo), also available on Amazon, for about $20. It is only 8" X 8" and weighs just a couple of pounds (see Essential Gear section).

To weigh items using a luggage scale, place all the items to be shipped into a box. Fashion a "sling" or strap of sorts by tying bags from retail stores together. Place the sling around the box with the merchandise, and attach it to the hook of the luggage scale. Lift the box, and *voilá* – you have your shipping weight.

Be creative here and use what is at your disposal. You could fashion a sling from hotel towels, sheets, or even packing tape. Just be sure to subtract the weight of the towels, sheets, or other improvised item that you use. If you have a belt, or have the forethought to bring a strap with you, then by all means use that.

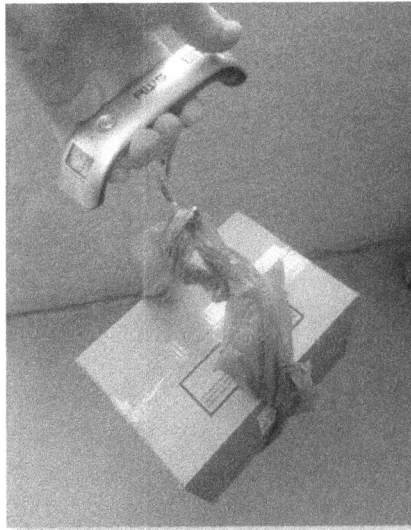

Getting Box Weight Using Sling Made from Tied Plastic Grocery Bags

My preference is to travel light, and improvise as needed. Improvised solutions are strangely satisfying. If you use the Design Go Travel Trolley (http://amzn.to/1mcXrFr) (see Essential Gear section), you can place your box of items on it, and then hook the luggage scale onto it to get your box weight. Remember to weigh and then deduct the weight of the travel trolley (about 3 pounds) to get an accurate final weight.

The aforementioned scales are affordable options that I have personally vetted, and they meet my criteria of being compact, lightweight, and functional. There are myriad other brands and models of scales available on Amazon

– they don't call it "earth's largest selection" for nothing! There are also models available in local retail stores. Get what suits you and your situation best. I do not recommend analog scales. They are often very inaccurate. I learned this the hard way, with weight readings off by 100% in some cases. Talk about cutting into margins!

HOW DO I PRINT LABELS, PACKING SLIPS, ETC.?

Sigh…another non-issue. Isn't it amazing how fear has the potential to keep us stagnant? Wherever you may be, there is likely a library, or a hotel with a business center, or an Internet café. All of these are places where you can print! You can also print using a thermal printer and a laptop or netbook (more on this later).

Most libraries are very accommodating, granting visitor's passes (usually free) for temporary use of their computers/Internet/printers. The printing costs are nominal; usually 10 cents per page. If you're staying at a hotel with a business center, you can usually print unlimited copies, as a benefit of being a guest. Internet cafes are more common than ever, and often have printing capabilities for a fee. Many UPS stores and Staples also have printing capacity, but they usually are a bit more costly. The key is to remain flexible and look for solutions wherever you find yourself.

I used to use Amazon's "stickerless commingled inventory" option, as it seemed to be the path of least resistance, and was especially appealing while traveling. How do you deal with labeling items? Don't label them at all! Or so I thought. There are risks with this strategy: Since your merchandise is being commingled with that of other merchants, you will be liable for any defects of other merchant's merchandise. For example, if you sent in a product with an expiration date (e.g., cosmetics, nutritional supplements, gourmet food items, etc.), you may have done everything right, but because the inventory is commingled, your customer may get an item that is expired (or worse - damaged), and you get the negative feedback.

However, you can still get away with not labeling items by using Amazon's labeling service. This saves time, which is often fleeting while traveling. It costs 20 cents per item, but it saves you from having to carry labels with you, load them into a printer at a hotel or library, and then place them on all of your products.

WHERE DO I STAGE ITEMS FOR SHIPPING?

You can find some space in your hotel room, or use the bed. Just be creative. If you have too much stuff, you can leave some of it in the car (if you have one) and move things in and out in stages, until you have it all packed and ready to ship.

If you're on foot, you can usually arrange with the manager of the store where you just bought a ton of stuff, to pick it up later after you figure out the logistics. I use the "Ready, Fire, Aim" approach. It's pulling the trigger without overanalyzing. If you overanalyze, chances are you won't make much progress and you may fail to take action at all. No action equals no profit!

If you're going to analyze, analyze why you're fearful of taking action. Fear comes from uncertainty/insecurity. If you're using your scouting tools correctly, you should be able to keep fear at bay and act decisively after you scan an item. If you're new to this game, fear is normal and beneficial; it will prevent you from becoming reckless. As you gain experience, you will become more confident, and fear will fade away.

WHAT DO I USE FOR PACKING MATERIAL?

The simple answer: Use all those plastic retail bags that previously held the merchandise you just bought. Put your items into each box, and then fill the empty space with wadded-up plastic retail bags.

Another option is a box resizer tool, to cut the box to get rid of empty space, making packing material unnecessary. You can accomplish roughly the same thing with a pair of scissors and a straight-edge, such as a box edge, or a scrap of cardboard. Also, you can often pack the box full without the need for packing material at all, provided the items fit closely together.

WHAT TIME DOES MY FLIGHT LEAVE, AND DO I HAVE ENOUGH TIME TO PACK AND SHIP?

Keep an eye on that clock! This is crunch time, and it can get hectic. As a last resort, if your flight is looming and you have not processed everything for FBA, throw the remaining items into a box and ship it to your home address. This is not ideal, since you will incur additional shipping costs (both to your house, and then again when you ultimately ship them to Amazon), negatively impacting your margin and adding to your workload, but it beats leaving things behind or returning them to the store. (Which is probably impractical, since your flight is leaving soon!)

Yet another option is a relatively new service provided by My Inventory Team (https://www.myinventoryteam.com/). With this service, you can send your inventory to their warehouse where it is prepared and shipped to Amazon on your behalf. There are fees associated with their services, but this may be a feasible solution.

Alternatively, if the items are small enough, you may be able to take some of them back with you in your carry-on or checked luggage. I have done this many times without issue. Consider bringing an empty carry-on bag (such as a large duffel bag) with you for this purpose.

DID I LEAVE THE STOVE ON, BACK HOME?

Sometimes we let irrational fears consume our thoughts. A lot of what we fear never comes to fruition. Focus your attention on productive thoughts and activities, and you will find you have fewer irrational fears consuming your thoughts.

If after you've breathed deeply, practiced a few asanas, and eaten an organic breakfast, you are still worrying, call your neighbor back home and ask whether your house is still standing or has been reduced to ashes. This will set your mind at ease, unless, of course, you really did leave the stove on, and the house was reduced to ashes (then you'll have a whole host of other things to worry about). But for now, you can only focus on the task at hand, which is shipping profitable items to FBA, so get to it – your flight leaves in a few hours!

CREDIT CARD MAGIC (USING NONE OF YOUR OWN MONEY TO BUILD AN EMPIRE)

WARNING, DISCLAIMER, ETC.

This strategy involves risk, responsibility, and accountability. There is no guarantee your items will sell! However, if you're a proficient scout, and you price your items competitively, the benefits should outweigh the risks, resulting in more wins than losses. If you lack discipline, or are not good at planning, I **DO NOT** recommend this strategy. Instead, just use a single card, and limit your expenditures to what you are confident you can handle, supported by your monthly sales. Or, don't use credit at all. (It's hard to believe, but there was a time when credit cards didn't exist, and somehow humanity survived.) If you get in over your head with credit card debt, you will have to change course, and likely pay some finance charges. Now for the strategy…

What's better than making huge returns on your money? Making huge returns on other people's money, and reaping the benefits for yourself. It's possible to structure your credit cards with staggered closing dates, which will also stagger your due dates. Using this strategy, you will have as much as 60 days' use of other people's money (the bank's) while you are profiting off of it, by selling items on Amazon.

To do this, you need at least two credit cards, but preferably three, or more. For example, with three cards, you would structure your closing dates spaced 10 days apart, on the first, 10th and 20th of the month. Write the closing and due dates on a slip of paper and tape it to the back of each card, for easy reference.

To fully leverage the benefits of this strategy, you simply begin using the card immediately *after it has closed*, and avoid using your other cards. As the month progresses, you use the next card, just after the closing date, and stop using the previous one.

Card	Closing Date	Begin Using
1	1st day of month	2nd day of month
2	10th day of month	11th day of month
3	20th day of month	21st day of month

Maximizing Credit Card Float

By using a card immediately after the closing date, you have until the next closing date of the following month before the charges are due. Then you will receive your statement, which is typically due in approximately another 30 days, though this will vary with each card issuer. This lag time is known as "float" and it can be very advantageous to your business.

Note that I said you have use of the bank's money for **UP TO 60 days**. It is impossible for me to know exactly how long you will have, since the process varies for each bank. However, it is usually 30-45 days at a minimum. Can you sell items on Amazon in 30-45 days? You betcha!

Another benefit of this strategy is that you don't get a mammoth credit card bill all at once. Consider that if you charged $6,000 on one card, you would get one $6,000 credit card bill. If you use the aforementioned strategy, you would have spent the same amount of money, but you divided the expenses into more manageable installments that you are more likely to be able to repay, because you're making sales on Amazon the entire time. In my book (which you're reading) it is a lot easier to divide $6,000, writing checks in three installments, rather than writing one huge one.

This is the exact strategy I used to grow my Amazon inventory to 1,500 items in my first two months, and I can say unequivocally that the plan works, if you work the plan. If I had not been able to use credit cards to leverage the bank's money, when I began, it would have taken me much longer to be successful with FBA.

Rapid success comes from building your inventory level quickly. The more inventory you have, the more you can sell, and the more you sell, the more your business grows, resulting in more profits. If you don't build momentum quickly, you're likely to not build it at all; it's just the nature of things.

Yet another benefit of using credit cards to build your business is that you get all kinds of perks from the card companies. Mileage, cash back, bonus merchandise, hotel discounts, free lodging, etc. These make sense only if you are able to pay your balances without accruing finance charges. Otherwise, the finance charges quickly outweigh the benefits.

FUNDING YOUR TRAVELS

You could theoretically travel perpetually, using these strategies to support yourself. Let's explore some ways you can make this a reality.

RV TRAVEL

There is an entire culture of RV enthusiasts who travel to swap meets, flea markets, etc., selling merchandise to support themselves as they go along. Amazon trumps any swap meet or flea market with the sheer volume of both its inventory and customer base (11 million and 225 million, respectively). If you're already living the RV lifestyle, Traveltage could be an ideal business model for you.

RVs are not cheap to own or maintain. They also aren't known for their great gas mileage. If you choose to go this route, closely analyze the associated costs. If you spend hundreds of dollars in fuel and other costs, you'll need to make significantly more than that to cover your expenses, and still make a profit from your Traveltage endeavors. It may make more sense to travel via other means, and then use the money you would otherwise spend on an RV for inventory or other travel expenses. Consider renting an RV and taking it for a test drive. This will allow you to see if this approach will suit your needs.

A viable alternative to an RV is an SUV (or van) which gets better gas mileage, has cargo space, and possibly provides bare bones living quarters. You might also consider adding a cargo or travel trailer if you need additional space.

Ideally, strive to be nimble and efficient, shipping most or all of what you find as soon as possible. It just doesn't make sense, nor is it practical to be accumulating and traveling with merchandise. Find it, pack it, ship it (and do it quickly) to minimize hassles. If you decide to go this route, consider that you might be able to deduct as business expenses:

- The RV itself
- Maintenance
- Fuel
- Mileage
- Smartphone
- Meals

Since there are scouting opportunities almost everywhere, you could theoretically deduct EVERY expense while practicing Traveltage. However, check with qualified professionals to assess your particular situation.

ALL ABOARD THE TRAVELTAGE TRAIN

If you have an aversion to flying, want a scenic route to a destination, or time is not a major factor in your travel plans, trains are a possibility. Recently I boarded an Amtrak train to explore the country while using Traveltage to pay for the trip along the way. I was excited to try this approach, but sadly, my first experience was not a good one.

The train was three hours late. If I had flown I would have already arrived at my destination in those lost three hours. When the train did finally arrive (delayed due to mechanical issues), I still had a 14 hour trip ahead of me. In total, my trip to Los Angeles took 17 hours — a trip that would have taken only three hours by plane. NOT the best use of my time. I could have flown to *New Zealand* in 17 hours, and no doubt found some very unique Traveltage items!

Train travel is admittedly out of favor in light of air travel. It flat out takes longer — *considerably longer* — to arrive at your destination via train versus flying. But, train travel can be very economical, beating virtually any other mode of transportation. Additionally, you can save lodging costs if you plan strategically. For instance, if you board the train at 5:00 PM, arriving at your destination the next morning, you have covered travel and lodging, but paid only for the travel. Let Amtrak do the driving, and you will awaken at your destination ready for a profitable day of Traveltage.

There are a few caveats though. In my experience, trains are frequently late. One reason for this is that passenger trains share the tracks with freight trains. Freight, being heavy, can only be transported at slow speeds, and if a passenger train gets behind a freight train, it must slow down.

An Amtrak route from Chicago to Los Angeles takes 39 hours under the best of conditions. Throw in a few unforeseen circumstances along the way, and it's no surprise that trains are often late. The savings for single tickets on Amtrak is often nominal in comparison to flying, especially considering the drastic difference in travel time. However, if you choose train travel, the most economical way to go is by using Amtrak's "USA Rail Passes," which are available in 15, 30, and 45 day allotments.

Here's an overview:

Pass (days)	Cost	Segments
15	$429	8
30	$649	12
45	$829	18

Amtrak USA Rail Pass Overview

A "segment" is defined as embarking to, or disembarking from the train. Assuming you purchase a USA Rail Pass, you could go straight from Chicago to Los Angeles for approximately $50, using just one of the segments on your rail pass! But, you might have more fun (and discover more Traveltage opportunities) by stopping in Kansas City, Albuquerque, Flagstaff, or any of the other stops along the way. Once in Los Angeles, you could then use another segment to travel up the Pacific Coast, and so on.

Keep in mind that the clock starts ticking as soon as you begin traveling. You must use your segments within the allotted days on the pass, or you will forfeit the unused portion. The pass expires 180 days after purchase. And, of course, you need to save some segments to get back home! More info here (http://bit.ly/1gVPe9K).

There are definitely pros and cons to train travel. Assess whether this is something that works for your particular situation. Given the huge time investment, I cannot wholeheartedly recommend this as a viable method for Traveltage. Instead, pay a bit more for a flight, and use the massive time savings productively, to source more products, which should defray the additional cost of the flight.

ULTIMATE SELF-SUFFICIENCY: YOUR MOBILE SHIPPING STATION

Whether you rent a car, or drive your own, you can literally do anything you need to in a parking lot, or on the side of the road. With a power inverter, you can run your laptop and your label printer anywhere you find yourself.

I recommend the Bestek 150 Watt inverter (Model MRI1511C) (http://amzn.to/1lHJ3lF) because, unlike many similar inverters that are available, it has a 2.1 Amp USB connection. Why is this important? Because the typical 1 Amp connection available on most models will take much longer to charge a laptop or cell phone.

The inverter can be used to power other items as well, but don't try anything too power hungry. If you exceed the rated 150 Watts you have a good chance of blowing a fuse, or melting wires. Laptops and label printers use a tiny amount of power. Combined, mine use only 40 Watts.

Bestek MRI1511C Power Inverter: The Key to the Traveltage Kingdom

Mobile Command Center: Laptop and Printer Attached to Bestek Power Inverter

LOGISTICS OF TRAVELTAGE

Once you arrive at your destination, you will need to find your way in your new surroundings. Depending on the city, traditional means of getting around such as bus or taxi will be available. You may also consider renting a car. If you will be in the city a while, make your lodging arrangements at a hotel and use it as your home base. Then hit the town!

SOURCING STRATEGIES

When you're in a store and you find products with the perfect combination of amazing margin plus limited supply on Amazon, it's a no-brainer to buy everything you can; but you're limited to what the store has on hand, especially in the case of clearance items. This is usually the end of the story…or is it? Politely ask the manager to check on-hand stock at other stores in the area. Even more politely, ask for a printout of the stores and quantities. Then create a plan to get the loot! To this end, I have successfully followed two main strategies:

Strategy 1:

Go to each store personally, and find the items—not always the easiest or most efficient way, but it can be very lucrative. If it's a store that you frequent, such as Walgreens, you will no doubt find other items that you know you can resell profitably, which you can snap up in your quest for the coveted items on your list. It's the proverbial "two birds with one stone."

My approach is to enter all the stores into my Magellan GPS, and then optimize the route to save time and gas. Incidentally, I prefer a dedicated GPS (the type that mounts to your dashboard or windshield) over the one on my smartphone, because they're easier to use than a smartphone while driving, and they typically have more features. While you're at it, be sure you have a dual outlet adapter that fits the car's cigarette lighter, so you can charge your phone and power the GPS at the same time.

Once on site, I quickly survey the store to see if I can locate the items myself. If so – it's a done deal. If not, with product list in hand I ask an employee, preferably a manager, for assistance. I say something on the order of:

> "I was just at your store on Clark St., and the manager was kind enough to run this report for me. It says your store has eight of these in stock. Do you know where they might be?"

It's important to point to the items in the list as you say this. This helps to overcome common tendencies of employees who feel this is not in their job description, and who might have a litany of excuses to avoid exerting effort on your behalf. When you hold a company-generated document that shows on-hand stock, there's generally no equivocation. Try it; it works!

If this seems obvious, that's because it is! But your competition is unlikely to go to this level of effort. I have done this multiple times, sourcing items that have netted me much more than my costs. These items often sell briskly on Amazon since they are often in short supply, thereby increasing their demand. You may find that you can use a "Blue Ocean" strategy (http://amzn.to/Rh1s0f) (see recommended reading), resulting in you being the only seller and thus commanding a premium for your items. Not bad for a little extra legwork!

Naturally, not everything will go as planned. Everyone would love it if everything they shipped sold immediately. Reality check: it's not going to happen. However, if you choose correctly more often than not, you'll be profitable.

In instances where inventory stagnates, run it through your scouting app again to see if there is an explanation for why it's not selling. Has another seller undercut your price so much that you're no longer in the running? Adjust accordingly, or don't. It depends on your personal business philosophy, as well as the market factors.

Ideally, you want your inventory to sell as quickly as possible so you get paid, of course, but also so you can use the revenue to pay your credit cards and reinvest in more inventory. By selling quickly, you also avoid short-term and long-term storage fees. Besides, it's just more fun to get those "Amazon has shipped the item you sold" emails, than not.

Strategy 2:

My preference is to use Strategy 1 when practical, because it yields great results, and I find I get less of a run-around from staff. But if the item is profitable enough to warrant my time and effort, but for some reason circumstances preclude me from physically going to the store, I simply call the store.

Again, obvious, right? Call the store and use a script similar to the one outlined in Strategy 1. Because you're not physically present, you'll likely encounter all manner of excuses. Retail stores aren't accustomed to customers calling to buy their entire stock of an item, so they often don't have a protocol to handle this type of inquiry. It's easier for them to get you off the phone than to deal with the logistics of getting merchandise to a distant customer. Nevertheless, persistence generally pays off.

Make it as easy and attractive for them as possible. Say something on the order of:

> "I was just at your store on Clark St., and the manager was kind enough to run this report for me for item "X." It says your store has twenty of these in stock. I'm in (insert name of town) and can't make it to your store. I will buy all twenty of them and pay by credit card if you can ship them to me." Note the similarities and differences to the first script. The extra detail is necessary to overcome likely objections.

In a perfect world you wouldn't encounter objections, because after all, the store exists to sell stuff, and they should be happy you're taking stagnant merchandise off their hands. But my experience has been otherwise.

If they balk at shipping the items to you, emphasize that you're willing to pay the cost of shipping. If they still won't budge, ask if they have a courier who can deliver the items to a store that is more convenient for you to pick up the items. Sometimes, there is an employee that lives near your town, but commutes to more distant stores. A district manager will periodically travel to the stores in the area and may be able to bring the items to a store nearer to you. In essence, emphasize that they have stuff to sell and you want to buy it! Ultimately, that should go a long way toward overcoming any objections.

CHAPTER 3

IDEAS TO ENHANCE TRAVELTAGE

My goal is to open your eyes to the opportunities available by practicing the art of Traveltage. There are many ideas that are beneficial but don't quite qualify as Traveltage, per se. Nonetheless, I felt they were too important to leave out, and they are as follows.

EFFICIENT BOX PACKING

Aside from sourcing, I find that packing boxes takes the most time. It's further compounded by not being efficient. After spending plenty of time inefficiently, I resolved to find a better way.

Here are a few tips:

Use Amazon's Scan & Ship feature, or a third party application like ScanPower, to list, and label your inventory.

Another logistical issue you will encounter is the distribution of your shipments to multiple warehouses. These multiple shipments are the bane of every Amazon seller's existence, resulting in seemingly illogical split shipments when all we really want is to make a single shipment to a single warehouse! Amazon's rationale for this, however, is perfectly logical. They are distributing inventory across multiple warehouses so that they can most efficiently ship it to the customer who purchases it. If all of your inventory is in a single warehouse on the East Coast, for instance, and someone from the West Coast orders it, it will take longer to get it to them. But if your inventory is in several warehouses across a wide geographic region, Amazon can send it from the warehouse nearest to the customer. They have the customer's best interest at heart, not the merchant's!

This annoying phenomenon can be minimized (but not entirely eliminated) with the Scan & Ship feature (called "Scan & Label" in some instances), which allows shipping to a single warehouse in many cases (more on this later). Note that Amazon only supports Scan & Ship on PCs. Macintosh users will need to use a program such as Parallels (http://amzn.to/1nykuds) to be able to use it. A Windows-based PC such as a netbook, which can be purchased very inexpensively, is another alternative.

Amazon has recently introduced an option called "inventory placement," which allows you to ship all of your items to a specific warehouse, however there are fees associated with this which may make it unfeasible. Assess whether the additional fees are something you're willing to absorb when deciding to use this service.

Sort your inventory in the Amazon "Manage FBA inventory" module.

See those headings at the top of each column? Clicking on them allows you to sort your inventory just like a spreadsheet. If you click the "Title" column, for instance, your inventory is sorted alphabetically. This is more efficient than going through your list in its default view, which is haphazard at best. You can use the same principles on the other columns – such as "Unfulfillable" – to quickly find your unfulfillable items, and send an email to Amazon to reimburse you and remove them from inventory, so you're not paying for dead weight.

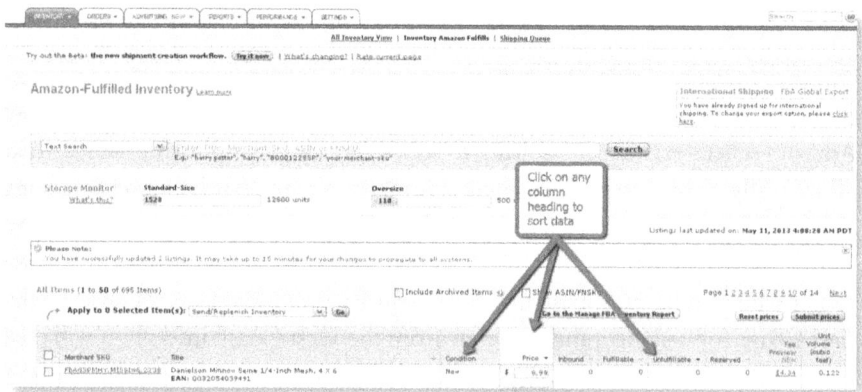

Sorting by Column Heading

Use the "add to shipment" feature of Profit Bandit, or other scouting apps.

To deal with the massive accumulation of merchandise that an active Traveltager amasses, efficiency is paramount. The "add to shipment" feature of Profit Bandit is absolutely brilliant. It allows you to build your shipment as you're scouting, then export it as a CSV (Comma Separated Values) file, which you can use to rapidly enter inventory into the Amazon system and get those products to FBA as soon as possible.

SALES STRATEGIES FOR MAXIMUM TURN TIMES AND RETURN ON INVESTMENT

One of the most important aspects of successful selling on Amazon is to price your offerings properly. Price too high and your inventory stagnates. Price too low and you leave money on the table, eroding your profits.

Pricing is an ongoing challenge. Since the Amazon marketplace is always in flux, you're basing crucial buying decisions on a moment in time, with the best data at your disposal from your scouting app at the time you scan it. But, after you ship the item to FBA, the market will change, and you may find that you are holding an item that isn't selling as well as you initially thought it would.

What to do? Use repricing software, such as ScanPower Repricer (http://bit.ly/1pirvAj), or Repriceit (http://bit.ly/1vQrqs2), among others, to remain competitive. If you are hopelessly under water, and other sellers are selling at or below your cost, you can create a removal order and have the items shipped back to you. At this point you could return them to the retailer, if you're still within the return period. However, strive to avoid this as much as possible, since returning items is not a good use of your time.

If someone has an item listed at or below your cost, and you simply can't afford to take a loss, you could hold out, but you may be waiting a long time, and in the meantime, you could be investing in more profitable items with better sales prospects. You'll have to assess each item on a case-by-case basis and then either discount your item for a quicker sale, or process a removal order.

If you decide to process a removal order you have the option to have the items shipped back to you at a cost of 50 cents per item or have them destroyed for 15 cents per item. There are instances where either solution makes sense, but this is personal preference and will be dictated by your business philosophy.

If I don't think the item is worth further time/effort, I opt to have Amazon destroy it. This results in a loss for me, but 15 cents is very nominal to remove the item from my inventory and avoid paying additional storage fees. If I think the item can be resold elsewhere or otherwise has some utility value to me, I opt for the 50 cents to have it returned to me.

PRINTING

If it weren't for the need to print packing slips and labels (and those meddling kids), you could run your entire FBA business from your smartphone. Always up for a challenge, I attempted to do exactly this. I *prefer* to use a laptop/ netbook and hand-held USB scanner when available, for reasons of efficiency and practicality, but it's nice to know that aside from printing, you can do everything from your smartphone.

Actually, you *can* print from your smartphone, too, though there are challenges, and it may not be practical in many situations.

I tested several printing apps. The app that I prefer is PrinterShare Mobile Print, which is available for both Android and iPhone. There is a one-time fee which at the time of this writing is $12.95.

Most mobile phone printing apps use Bluetooth, or Wi-Fi (Note that they do NOT print over a 3G/4G network in most instances. You must have access to a wireless LAN), and allow you to print to a wireless enabled printer. Go to Traveltage.com/bonus-downloads/ for a free walk-through of the printing process using PrinterShare Mobile Print.

When not traveling, I find that individual item labels are best printed on a dedicated thermal label printer, and packing slips and UPS labels are best printed on a laser printer. This combination yields the most economical use of printing supplies and the most efficient use of time. However, when traveling, you probably won't have the luxury of both a thermal printer and a laser printer, so you will need to compromise.

Ultimately, you may choose to have Amazon do the labeling for you, depending on your time constraints, budget, and proclivity toward labeling items. If so, you may not need a printer whatsoever. If you do choose to get a printer, ideally, it would be a "one stop" solution used to print individual item labels, and shipping labels. I set out with that goal in mind, and found it to be a challenge to achieve this using only a thermal printer, but I did find a suitable solution.

Direct thermal printers are a great choice because they provide an economical printing solution since they do not require ink cartridges. There's also less to go wrong with them; they typically have a long, maintenance-free lifespan. Because of these factors, thermal printing is reliable, efficient, and downright cheap!

As much as I love thermal printers, there are a few drawbacks. The main one is that they require thermal media for printing; you can't just use any paper. UPS provides free 4″ X 6″ thermal labels (item # 01774006) for account holders, and these work for many thermal printers (e.g., Zebra). These will NOT work in Brother or Dymo printers since these printers require proprietary media.

Labels are expensive if purchased from the printer manufacturers themselves, but can be very economical, if purchased from third party vendors.

A thermal printer is more lightweight and compact than a laser printer, so it's the obvious choice. I tested the Zebra LP-2844, Dymo 4XL and the Brother QL-1050 and found the Brother QL-1050 to be the best choice for Traveltage.

BROTHER QL-1050 PRINTER

The Brother QL-1050 (http://amzn.to/1hfvhW3) is the closest I've found to a one-stop printing solution, allowing the Traveltager to be completely self-sufficient. It is my top choice for ease of use, durability, and features. It can print 4″ X 6″ labels, and many other dimensions, too, due to its simple but ingenious design which allows different label dimensions to be switched quickly. Another excellent feature is the automatic label cutter.

You can print UPS labels (note that they will be formatted across two pages of 4″ X 6″ thermal stock versus the standard single 8-1/2″ X 11″ page), and labels for individual items.

The only drawback with this printer is that it uses proprietary label stock. There's no practical way around this, as the media itself has printed guide marks on the back, which the printer uses to align the labels.

Both die-cut and continuous label stock rolls are available, but I prefer the continuous rolls. Occasionally, you may need to create a custom label dimension for an item, and continuous roll media allows you to do so.

The rolls contain 100 feet of label stock, and are sold in various widths. A common product label size for Amazon is 1″ X 2-5/8″. At these dimensions, you can print 1,200 product labels from a single continuous roll. The label stock for the Brother printer is actually 2-3/7″ wide, which for all intents and purposes is the same as 2-5/8″. These rolls sell for about $3 each. That's 1/4 of a cent per label, or four labels for a penny. Not bad!

Of the printers I tested for Traveltage purposes, the QL-1050 (http://amzn.to/1hfvhW3) is the only one that can use continuous label stock (as opposed to die-cut label stock). Essentially the stock is one long 100 foot label that is custom cut to the desired length, as needed.

The rolls are available with or without the cartridge. I recommend and use the ones without the cartridge because the cost savings is substantial. To use these, and take advantage of the tremendous cost savings, you will initially need to buy a cartridge to hold the rolls of label stock. This is a one-time purchase, as the cartridge is reusable. The nominal cost enables you to use the least expensive label stock possible.

The only caveat with this printer is that it may not be compatible with several third party shipping solutions such as Stamps.com, Shiprush, UPS.com and USPS.com. This may be a consideration if you intend to use this printer for merchant-fulfilled orders, or other business needs not confined to FBA. If this is a significant concern for you, a Zebra or Dymo printer may be a better choice because of their more widespread industry usage.

Go to Traveltage.com/bonus-downloads/ for a free set up document to help you configure the printer for optimal use with FBA.

Brother QL-1050 Supplies

You can find these labels at the links below, or use the Brother stock numbers in parentheses to find other sources.

4″ Continuous Label Roll (DK-2243) and Reusable Cartridge (http://bit.ly/1vQs3lv)

2-3/7″ Continuous Label Roll (DK-2205) and Reusable Cartridge (http://bit.ly/Rh2lpz)

If it weren't for the pesky Amazon UPS label which is output as a PDF file formatted exclusively for 8-1/2″ X 11″ paper, all of your Amazon FBA printing needs could be easily handled by a thermal printer. But if you try printing something formatted 8-1/2″ X 11″ on 4″ label stock, you will run into all manner of problems.

But there is still a way! The UPS PDF file provided by Amazon must be split so that it fits the width of the label stock. This involves an additional step that is not necessary when printing to a laser printer, and can be accomplished with a utility called APDF Page Cut. The free version (http://bit.ly/1t1trNT) adds a demo watermark which requires purchasing the upgrade (http://bit.ly/1k0Kvhx) to remove.

The process is as follows:

1. Download the Amazon UPS PDF file as you normally would.

2. Open the PDF file in APDF Page Cut.

3. Split the label into two equally-sized images.

   a. Click: **Action > Add Horizontal Line**

   b. Click: **Cut and Save As**

4. Open the separated images and print them on the thermal printer.

5. Affix the labels to your package.

You will need to experiment with this. Expect to waste some label stock while getting the hang of it.

This is admittedly not an ideal solution, as it does take extra work and time, but it's a small price to pay to be able to process your shipments solely with a thermal label printer. If you have many labels to print, you can use the batch print feature to expedite the process.

HOW TO PROCESS INVENTORY AND SHIPMENTS WITHOUT A PRINTER

You really can run your FBA business almost entirely from your smartphone. The scouting portion is handled with apps such as ScanPower Scout, Profit Bandit, etc. The inventory entry and shipping is handled within the Amazon FBA console, or third party software such as ScanPower.

Each of the sub-sections of the process flow within the Amazon FBA console can be skipped and revisited at any time. You might not be aware of this, since there is usually no need to deviate from the process flow as Amazon lays it out for you. But the logistics of travel sometimes necessitate that you stray from the normal process flow.

While working from a hotel room, RV, etc., you can complete the entire process of listing and packing your inventory, and then print labels later when you have access to a printer.

You can click on any of the following headings in the Amazon process flow to view information or to make modifications:

- Set Quantity

- Select Carrier

- Prepare Shipment

- Provide Details

- Label Shipment

- Summary

If you don't have access to a printer, simply skip the "Prepare Shipment" and "Label Shipment" sections, and revisit them later when you do.

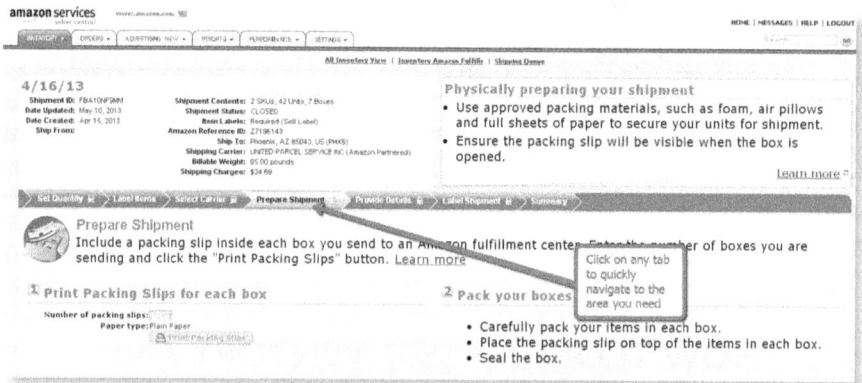

Navigating the FBA Process Flow

CHAPTER 4

ADVANCED TECHNIQUES AND THE FINER POINTS OF TRAVELTAGE

I found myself (though not in a spiritual way) in Denver, CO, on Memorial Day. I found some great bargains and intended to follow my usual Traveltage technique of printing at a local library. However, the libraries were closed for the Memorial Day holiday! To make matters worse, I also realized that I had forgotten my scale on this particular trip. I was stuck, but ultimately came up with this solution:

First, I entered everything into my inventory on my smartphone, and then found a nearby Staples store where I took my boxes of merchandise to be weighed. While they were being weighed, I struck up a conversation with the kind sales associate:

> **Me:** "I don't suppose there's a way I could print here, is there?"
>
> **Her:** "Well, if you have a USB flash drive, you can save your documents to it using one of our laptops on the sales floor, and then bring the file here so we can print it for you."
>
> **Me:** "Holy $&%#, this just has to go in my Traveltage book!"

I proceeded to one of the myriad laptops for sale on the sales floor, connected my USB flash drive, logged in to my Amazon account, and saved the PDFs of the shipping labels and packing slips. I then gave the flash drive to the sales associate, who printed them. I put the packing slips in the boxes, sealed them, affixed the shipping labels, and it was off to the races.

The implications of this are astounding! You can go into any city armed with only a smartphone and USB flash drive, and make this business work! Ideally, you would have a little more to work with: a laptop computer, USB barcode scanner, and a portable printer are nice additions that will make life easier and drastically speed up the process. Traveltage is a truly minimalistic business. It can be operated on a shoestring and is extremely flexible. No yoga required.

A LESSON IN EXTREME MINIMALISM (HOW TO DESTROY ANY VESTIGE OF EXCUSES THAT YOU CAN'T DO THIS)

On a recent trip to Santa Monica, CA, I set out to explore the surrounding area with no intention of practicing Traveltage. But, I find ubiquitous high profit items difficult to overlook. It seems almost sacrilegious to fail to take advantage of situations where items can be resold at 100-500% margins, or more. Once the Traveltage bug sinks its teeth into you, it doesn't let go, and thus I gave in to my addiction!

I boarded the #8 bus, and asked the bus driver where I might find a shopping center. She recommended the Sepulveda/National stop. Because I hadn't planned ahead, I was ill-prepared. Armed with nothing but my Android phone equipped with Profit Bandit, I wondered if I could pull this off. After stepping off the bus, I quickly surveyed the area, noting the following stores in a two-block radius:

- Ross
- Big Lots
- Rite-Aid
- CVS
- Staples
- Vons

I began at CVS and immediately found some excellent prospects:

Looking Good at CVS

First Haul of the Day at CVS

I then proceeded to Ross:

The Fun Continues at Ross

I bought 30 items. Because I didn't have my usual Traveltage items with me, here's what I had to buy to prepare the items for shipment:

- Packing Tape ($3)
- Rubbing Alcohol to remove retail price labels/adhesive ($2)
- Cotton cosmetic applicators/removers to remove retail price labels/adhesive ($2; I always like to look my best)
- Shipping boxes (Two each at $3; $6 total)
- 8GB USB flash drive ($8)
- Two packing slips and two FBA shipping labels printed at Staples (10¢ each; 40¢ total)
- Coconut water ($1.24, not for resale, but on clearance. What can I say? I'm a bargain shopper, and it was hot that day!)
- Lunch at Marie Callender's ($12, including tip)
- Bus fare of $2, round trip

As I walked into Staples with a full cart of merchandise from multiple retail stores, I couldn't resist quipping with the sales associate that I had "a few returns." My joke left the associate bewildered as he looked at my cart full of merchandise. No matter! Off to aisle 3 to buy boxes.

I proceeded to the back of the store. Taking a seat in a bonded leather chair, I sidled up to a faux walnut laminate desk and began preparing my newly purchased items for shipment to Amazon, in my newfound office away from home.

Impromptu Command Center at Staples

Using my smartphone, I began listing all the items I had purchased. I removed all the price stickers, and used rubbing alcohol and cotton cosmetic pads to remove residual adhesive. Since I didn't have access to a printer, I chose the Amazon labeling service option to label my items upon arrival at their warehouse. I changed my shipping address to the Staples National Blvd. address (to get accurate shipping rates), carefully packed the items into the boxes, and then proceeded to the shipping counter.

After getting accurate weights, I proceeded to the sales floor, purchased a USB flash drive, and logged into my Amazon account on one of the laptops for sale, just as I had done on my Denver trip. I attached the flash drive and saved the PDFs of the packing slips and FBA shipping labels. I then took the flash drive to the nice sales associate, who printed the PDFs. I affixed them to my packages and left them for UPS to pick up.

Several hours later (and after a relaxing lunch at Marie Callender's), I boarded the #8 and headed back to my hotel. I include this story to illustrate what's possible. You can literally make this business work practically anywhere, with nothing but your smartphone. I assume, however, that I would eventually have to start paying Staples for office space if I made a regular habit of this technique…It's always SOMETHING, now isn't it? Nonetheless, excuses be gone!

The total time spent, including scouting, preparing, packaging, and transit time on the bus could have been reduced significantly, had I planned ahead. I also could have been more efficient if I'd had my USB barcode scanner and netbook, as well as my Traveltage supplies already with me. You can certainly do everything you need to do using your smartphone alone, but for the sake of efficiency, you'll want to use other resources, as available.

As I left Staples, Marc Cohn's song "Walking in Memphis," was playing over the sound system. Hmmm…Memphis, maybe Traveltage will take me there next…

All that's left to say is:

Thanks Staples, that was easy!

TIME MANAGEMENT & EFFICIENCY

To be successful with Traveltage, and still have some time to explore and enjoy wherever you find yourself, you need to make the most of your time. Actually, this applies to life in general. There are many times when you find yourself waiting, and this otherwise "wasted" time can be channeled into productivity and ultimately, profitability.

Here are some ideas:

- Add items to inventory using your smartphone while waiting in line to check out. (This has the added benefit of preventing you from purchasing "hazmat" or restricted items which will become evident when you attempt to ship them to FBA).

- Source products and boxes for shipping simultaneously while in retail stores.

- Group like items together to quickly get counts for inventory and packing purposes.

- Remove price stickers while printing labels.

- Weigh, pack, seal, and label shipments during any downtime throughout the process.

- Export scanned items to a CSV (Comma Separated Values) file, to speed up the process of entering inventory into FBA.

Another aspect of time management and efficiency relates to how much time you spend entering inventory data, labeling inventory, monitoring inventory levels, and repricing inventory. There are several software applications that are available to streamline this process, and they are well worth considering if you want to maximize your profitability and avoid getting bogged down in menial, low return activities. Not to mention, you can have more fun and concern yourself less with the minutiae that might otherwise consume your day. I'm all for that!

AMAZON SCAN & SHIP

A little known and under-utilized feature that Amazon provides is "Scan & Ship." Find it here:

Inventory > Manage FBA Shipments > Scan & Ship

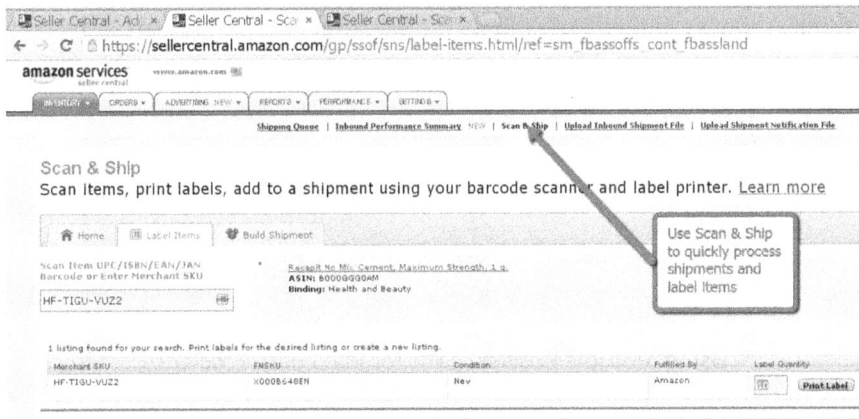

Using Scan & Ship

Scan & Ship allows you to print individual labels in the same fashion as many of the commercial applications, for free. With a handheld USB barcode scanner you can quickly prepare shipments.

As previously noted, Amazon only supports Scan & Ship on PCs. Macintosh users will need to use a program such as Parallels (http://amzn.to/1nykuds) to be able to use it. A Windows-based PC such as a netbook, which can be purchased very inexpensively, is another alternative.

Aside from the occasional item which inexplicably can't be processed using this feature, it's fast, simple, and effective.

When you do get the inevitable message that a particular item cannot be sent to the FBA warehouse for which you're currently preparing a shipment, set it aside and either process it using the normal Amazon process flow, or create a new shipment in Scan & Ship. If you opt for the latter, chances are good that you will be shipping to a different warehouse that will accept the item in question.

To maximize your efficiency, open multiple tabs in your browser, so you can quickly navigate between them. In this fashion, you can add the item to your inventory, print a label, and add an item to a shipment in quick succession.

For maximum flexibility, I prefer Google Chrome, but Firefox, and Internet Explorer should work as well. The first tab you open is the "Add product" tab, found here:

Inventory > Add Product

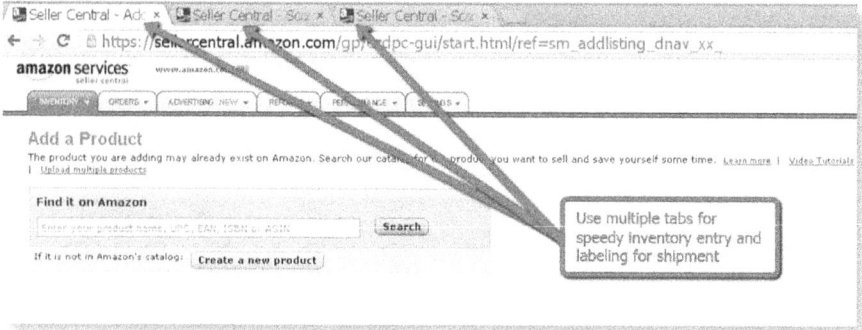

Using Multiple Browser Tabs for Maximum Efficiency

Use your barcode scanner to scan the UPC and find the item in Amazon's catalog. Open a second tab in the Scan & Ship area and click on the "Build Shipment" tab. Found here:

Inventory > Manage FBA Shipments > Scan & Ship

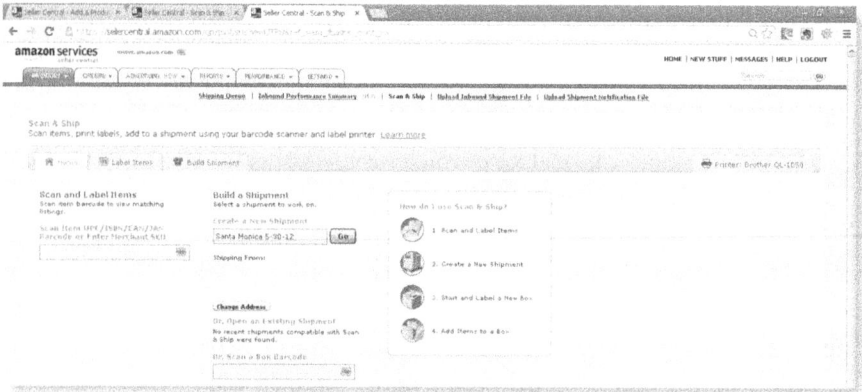

Scan & Ship Shipment Tab

Assign a name to the shipment and verify that the address you're shipping from is correct. Change the address as needed (when shipping from a new location) to ensure you get accurate shipping rates. Then click on the "Label Items" tab:

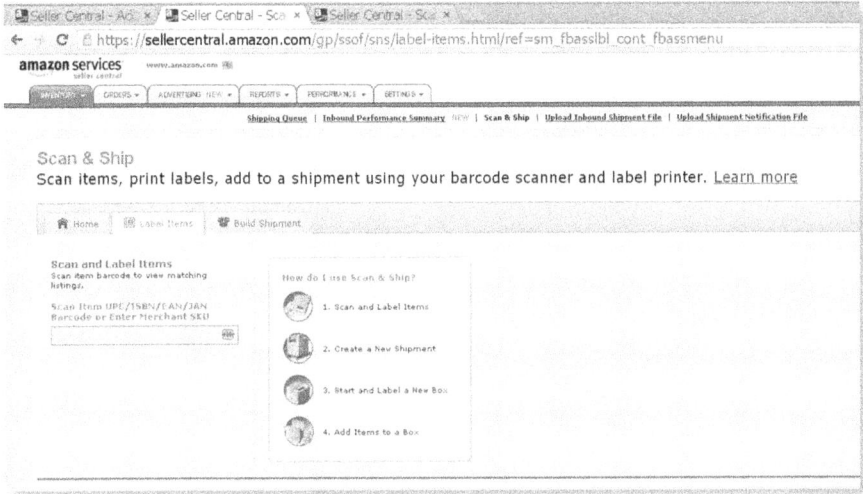

Scan & Ship Label Tab

Manually enter the item UPC or ASIN, or use your barcode scanner to scan the UPC. Note that you cannot label an item until it is in your inventory. This may seem obvious, but if an item isn't listed in your inventory before attempting to label it, the Scan & Ship application stares back at you blankly when you scan an item.

In addition to Scan & Ship, I use flat files which are provided by Amazon. The template that I use the most is "Inventory Loader," however, there are many to choose from, and you may consider using different ones based on the type of inventory you're working with. You can review and learn more about them here (http://amzn.to/1jJBG1n).

The templates are available here:

Inventory > Add Products Via Upload > Download Template

To upload them:

Inventory > Add Products Via Upload > Select Type of File to Upload

The Inventory Loader is useful for quickly loading items into your inventory (hence the name). You will need some technical aptitude and more than a little patience to use these spreadsheet templates. It took me many hours of trial and error to master them. Once I did, I found them to be great tools to help quickly process inventory and shipments. If you follow these steps, you can very efficiently label and prepare your shipments. Once you master flat files, you'll find there is no faster way to enter inventory. If time is short, consider using the labeling service provided by Amazon, as previously described. To enable the labeling service:

Settings > Fulfillment by Amazon > Optional Services > Label Service

Amazon designed this so you can opt out of the service on a case-by-case basis. Label your items yourself when it makes sense, and let Amazon do it when it doesn't. Nice!

CHAPTER 5

SOFTWARE AND APPS TO MAKE TRAVELTAGE EASIER

Some of the best resources available are completely free. Although you don't *need* anything other than free apps to succeed in this business, you will find that the paid apps offer more features and can speed up the scouting process significantly. That translates to more efficiency and better time management. You have only so much time on the planet. Use it wisely!

There are many useful apps available – actually, the marketplace is awash in them. I have narrowed the field to ones that I personally use and recommend. You can search the iPhone or Android marketplaces to find myriad others.

FREE APPS

Card Star

With this app, you simply scan all the barcodes of the frequent shopper card programs where you are a member, and it stores them in your smartphone. (Note there is similar functionality called "Passbook" built into iOS devices.) When you need them, there's no more hunting for the card; just pull up the barcode, and have the cashier scan it. An added bonus is that many of the retailers have special offers that they market this way. You might find some items to resell. Become a card star!

Shop Savvy

Shop Savvy is a shopping app designed for consumers to get the best price. The information isn't as comprehensive as a paid app, but it's still useful. If you don't have a paid scouting app you can use it to scout for deals.

UPS Mobile

This app helps you locate UPS shipping locations. Uncheck the option for "UPS Drop Box," to avoid going to a location that can't accommodate your shipment. Note that you can also ship from Staples and Office Depot, in addition to the UPS stores and customer centers you find using this app.

This app can also process shipments for pickup, which you can use to your advantage if you have a UPS account. Simply have your packages picked up from your location. Finally, it has tracking for packages. Very handy, and especially useful in a new location where you don't know the lay of the land.

INDIVIDUAL STORE APPS

There is an app for everything these days. Every retailer has one. These can be useful for locating stores and for special discount offers or sale notifications. Download one for Kohl's, Walgreens, CVS and any other store you can think of, and go nuts!

Amazon Price Check

This is a shopping app that can be used in lieu of a paid scouting app. While it lacks comprehensive information such as the sales rank, provided by paid apps, you can use this app to quickly ascertain the going rate of an item on Amazon. com. Quickly filter out non-FBA offers by clicking the "FREE Super Saver Shipping" box, so you are basing your buying decisions on offers currently listed by FBA sellers, and not merchant fulfilled offers.

Amazon Seller

At the time of this writing this app is only available for iPhone users. It has many of the features that apps like Profit Bandit and ScanPower have (e.g., Sales rank, number of competing offers, ability to list items for sale within app, etc.).

So what makes it any different than the myriad other scanning apps available? One key difference is a feature that lists Amazon Selling Restrictions. Using this feature, you can quickly tell if an item has restrictions or is unsellable on Amazon. This way you can avoid dealing with the dreaded "This item is restricted and cannot be sold on Amazon" message. Messages like this are particularly painful when you thought you got the deal of the century, only to find you're stuck with unsellable merchandise.

Another nice feature is the product reviews, which as far as I know, are not included in any other scanning app. At a glance you can tell the number and star rating of reviews. If an item is very poorly rated, you might think twice about choosing to sell it yourself.

At the time of this writing, this app is still under development. Pending additional features include:

- Inventory Management
- Order Management
- Sales Summary

Note that Amazon's "Net Proceeds" figures are not as comprehensive as ones from apps like Profit Bandit and ScanPower. You'll still need to factor in your cost to purchase, as well as inbound shipping.

PAID APPS

ScanPower Scout

This scouting tool, developed and supported by Chris Green and the staff of ScanPower, offers much more than free apps do, and includes useful information such as sales rank, as well as the ability to list the item for sale in your inventory on the spot. Your first five days of scanning are free. Thereafter, there is a $40/month recurring fee.

Profit Bandit

Profit Bandit is a sophisticated scouting tool that, in addition to providing sales rank and competing offers, allows you to export items to a CSV file for use with a spreadsheet. This allows for more rapid entry of shipments and higher efficiency. By tapping the sales rank or title of the item, you can search BookFinder, CamelCamelCamel, eBay, Google Products, PaperBackSwap, PriceGrabber and Pricewatch. If the item you're considering buying for resale isn't listed on Amazon, use one of these sites to get an idea of its value.

Another excellent feature of this app is that it allows you to list an item for sale directly on Amazon, from within the app. This is very handy and prevents purchasing resale items which may be restricted or considered "hazmat," and therefore cannot be sold via FBA. The developer charges a $9.99 monthly fee. I personally use this app and have found it does everything I require.

TAMING THE BOOKKEEPING BEAST

In my first month of sourcing products, I was shocked by how many receipts I accumulated. I had a disorganized stack several inches thick. With the whirlwind approach I took, I was preoccupied with sourcing and shipping hundreds of items to FBA. I couldn't be bothered with the mundane tasks associated with bookkeeping!

While enthusiastically discussing my FBA success with my girlfriend, she nonchalantly asked me what the bottom line numbers on my fledgling business venture were. I honestly didn't know. I just knew I was selling and shipping a lot of stuff at high margins. Why worry about anything else?

The dynamic nature of sourcing, shipping, and selling makes this a rapidly moving target that you can't easily put your finger on at any given moment. However, it is a business, after all, so keeping tabs on the numbers is a crucial fundamental that can't be ignored. On the road, it's even more important to have a system to keep track of everything, lest you get lost in a mountain of paperwork and find yourself painfully navigating it at tax time.

Here are a few solutions to tame the bookkeeping beast:

Godaddy Bookkeeping (Formerly Outright)

Godaddy Bookkeeping is specifically designed for online sellers. It synchronizes with your Amazon Pro Seller account, and calculates pertinent bookkeeping information. There is a free version as well as a premium version, for $9.95 per month. As you might imagine, the premium version offers more features than the free one. The free version, however, is extremely robust. Experiment with what works best for your business.

NeatReceipts

NeatReceipts is a package consisting of a specialized scanner and software designed specifically for managing receipts. You scan all your receipts, creating a digital copy. You can organize them to ease your record keeping. It's advisable to keep the original filed in a folder for safe-keeping. Since most receipts are printed using thermal technology, the print fades over time. This is another reason to have a digital copy available.

RECEIPT MANAGEMENT APPS

To truly be a Traveltage minimalist, you'll want to travel as light as possible. Leave all the equipment behind and just grab your smartphone, along with a few other essentials. To this end, if you search the Android and Apple marketplaces, you will find many receipt management solutions. They work by using the camera on your smartphone to scan your receipts, (just like the scouting apps) which are then securely stored, categorized, and accessible to you.

Using these apps, with just a few taps, your receipts are scanned quickly and efficiently, removing the onerous task of managing them via spreadsheets or other means. It takes just seconds to scan a receipt. You then have a reliable archive.

As an added bonus, you have a running total of your expenditures at any given moment. These apps are my preferred solution, as they free me up to focus on more profitable areas of the business, and they don't require any additional hardware.

Additionally, they have options to export data to various applications, or as CSV files, so you can import them into virtually any accounting software. Below are a few apps I recommend.

Shoeboxed

Shoeboxed (http://bit.ly/1nyn8jc) is a comprehensive solution which costs far less than a bookkeeper. Scan your receipts with your smartphone or desktop scanner, or take advantage of their service that allows you to send your receipts directly to them, and they will scan them for you. It's like Netflix for receipts. They send you envelopes. You send them your receipts. All scans are verified by humans, to ensure data integrity, since optical scanning technology is imperfect at best.

Shoeboxed integrates with many online bookkeeping solutions such as Outright, Freshbooks, Quickbooks, etc.

There is a free version of Shoeboxed available, but it is not practical for active FBA businesses, since you will exceed the limitations very quickly.

Their service is more expensive than many of the others; however, they offer more options and a higher level of customer service.

If you have a mountain of receipts to deal with, you will be ahead of the game by sending them all to Shoeboxed. Let them do the heavy lifting, while you focus on sourcing and shipping more products for your business (unless, that is, you enjoy the task of tracking receipts).

I asked Joel Bush, Vice President, Sales & Alliances, at Shoeboxed, the following questions:

Are there any safeguards in place to deal with receipts that might get lost in the mail, in transit to/from Shoeboxed?

"This is a great question. Our envelopes are postage-paid, pre-addressed, and made of Tyvek. We also intercept the mail at the regional postal processing center, so they do not go out for carrier delivery. Taking these factors into account, we are addressing 90+% of the reasons why mail gets lost (or destroyed, etc.). To-date we have never lost a Shoeboxed envelope. That said, many of our customers send us their documents via FedEx or UPS to ensure delivery. Or, if you have a scanner on your side, you can send your receipts to Shoeboxed via email, through the website, or by using our "Desktop Uploader" too, and never have to part with your documents."

Aside from not being able to physically mail receipts, and less streamlined integration with common online accounting applications, what other differences are there between you and your competitors?

"Beyond the submission options and the integration suite, the major differentiator between Shoeboxed and all other services similar to ours is the fact that we human-verify the extracted data. As you may know, OCR technology is typically 65-80% accurate - this simply isn't good enough if you are using our service to help get organized for taxes, or to populate an email marketing list."

LifeLock Wallet (Formerly Lemon)

The free version of LifeLock Wallet (http://amzn.to/1omUUt8) allows unlimited scans of receipts; however, I recommend updating to the premium plan.

The benefits of the premium plan are:

- Itemization of receipts for tax purposes
- Ability to export data to Evernote, Expensify, Box, Concur, or as a CSV file
- Comprehensive search features

They do not human verify receipts, nor do they provide the option to mail receipts to them, like Shoeboxed does. LifeLock Wallet is not as comprehensive as Shoeboxed, but if you're on a budget, this is a very good option. They are increasingly adding integration with online bookkeeping software. If yours isn't supported, simply export to a CSV file and import into your software of choice.

Expensify

Expensify's motto is "Expense Reports That Don't Suck." It works similarly to Shoeboxed and Lifelock Wallet with nearly identical functions and features, but adds mileage and hour tracking.

The free version allows unlimited scans, but requires you to manually enter some information. Their "SmartScan" technology automates the process, but is limited to 10 free scans monthly. Thereafter, the cost is 20 cents per SmartScan.

Expensify is optimized for Quickbooks, but it can export data in CSV format, for easy importing into other accounting software.

REPRICERS

Once you amass a large inventory, manually repricing it becomes an onerous task. A repricer will help you remain competitive with other seller's offers, and save you time by allowing you to reprice your items with minimal effort. There are many available. Here are a few with good reputations:

ScanPower Repricer

RepriceIt

CHAPTER 6

TRAVELTAGE MIND-SET

Traveltage presents unique challenges, many of which cannot be foreseen. That's OK, in fact, spontaneous events have a tendency to bring out the best in us, provided we don't lose our heads. You never know what you're capable of until you are required to rise up to overcome challenges.

The alternative is never being challenged, which usually results in boredom. Know that you can solve any problem that comes your way. Then, marshal your resources and overcome any obstacles preventing you from achieving your goal. With a little faith, determination, and belief in yourself, you will succeed.

TRAVELTAGE PRODUCT SOURCING GUIDELINES

Use the following criterion to help you make sourcing decisions:

Low sales rank

This will depend on the category of the item in question. A low sales rank in gourmet foods is quite different from toys or books. Generally speaking, I strive for sales ranks below 100,000. With items totaling 11 million (and growing) in the Amazon catalog, a sales rank of 100,000 ranks in the top 1% of products being sold. While there are no guarantees, and the ranks change hourly based on real-time sales data, lower sales ranks provide a higher likelihood of brisk sales than higher sales ranks. Given a sales rank of 100,000 (or less), or one that's closer to 11 million, the choice should be obvious.

High profit margin

This is a matter of personal taste and business philosophy, risk tolerance, etc. Generally you can go for margin or cash flow (and sometimes both). Maximum margin often (though not always) means waiting longer for the sale. Slimmer margins often result in quicker sales. I employ both strategies depending on the item and how other sellers are currently pricing their items.

Lightweight

If you're staying in a hotel, you will be carrying items to and from your hotel room, and potentially to and from the shipment location. With these considerations in mind, it's nice if things don't weigh a ton. For this reason, I shy away from books. Books are great, high margin items, but in bulk they are heavy! It's easy to amass a stack of books that weighs-in at 50 pounds; not my idea of fun, when I'm trying to navigate a new city. I prefer to source them only when I'm not on the road.

Small

I don't have anything against oversize items, as long as they have sufficient margin to cover the additional costs of shipping and storage at FBA warehouses. But oversize items often present additional logistical and packing challenges.

Back home, I usually like to have multiple oversize items before I ship, rather than shipping just one or two. I simply collect them until I have enough that warrants a shipment, but this not a luxury I have on the road. Therefore, I focus on smaller items that are easy to throw in a box and ship.

Besides, where are you going to get a box to accommodate that life-size Scooby Doo Funhouse, anyway? Like everything though, assess the situation, and if the margin is high enough, find a way to make it happen!

Durable

I wouldn't chance shipping fragile glass items from the road, regardless of the margin I could make on them. If they don't all end up smashed to bits on the way to FBA, there's a good chance they will on the way to the customer. This will create more work for you when you have to file a damage claim, or request that Amazon remove the inevitable negative feedback you will incur. You could avoid all this by simply choosing products that are not fragile. Come to think of it, this applies back home too, though if the margin warrants it, I will some-times take a chance, provided I can pack the items carefully.

Well-packaged from manufacturer

Many items will have a phenomenal profit margin, and be on the clearance shelves because the packaging has been opened/damaged. Avoid these types of items.

There are some items that have cutaways in the box, so the customer can feel the texture of an item, or test some of its features. Amazon best practices mandate that items such as these, with exposed fabric, for instance, be enclosed by plastic. On the road, you may not have access to plastic bags, or the item may be too large for bags that are readily available. However, in a pinch, you can use plastic wrap - the type used for covering food. Just wrap the item with the plastic wrap multiple times, pulling it tightly so it adheres to itself well. Tape it securely with clear packing tape, anywhere that it needs it. It won't look pretty, but it keeps the item from picking up dust and detritus during shipping and in FBA warehouses.

For a more professional appearance, I use a heat gun, after wrapping the item. If you happen to have a heat gun, you can get an appearance similar to shrink wrap. You may decide to forego purchasing items like this altogether, thereby avoiding the additional packing/shipping hassles that accompany them. This is certainly a viable option, and will be dictated by your preferences and business model.

Essential Gear

Here is a list of the items I never leave home without (unless I'm impulsively taking a random bus tour) when practicing Traveltage. As I compiled this list, I was struck by just how little is necessary to run this business. There aren't many businesses that can provide so many benefits for so little! More details for many of these items is available in the Traveltage Products section.

- American Weigh LS-110 Digital Luggage Scale (http://amzn.to/1jczvgN)
- Design Go Luggage Travel Trolley (http://amzn.to/1mcXrFr)
- Packing Tape (http://amzn.to/1lHLjtf)
- Clear UPS Envelopes (#171604) (http://bit.ly/1n91vYu)
- Child-Safe Blunt Nosed Scissors (http://amzn.to/1md32vq)

- Tape Measure (http://amzn.to/1tskRtr)
- Smartphone (http://amzn.to/1tskTSe) and Charger (equipped with Profit Bandit, or other scouting app, and Lemon or other receipt scanning app)
- Laptop (http://amzn.to/1ochnLU) or Netbook (http://amzn.to/1jcDolW)
- USB Flash Drive (http://amzn.to/TB0myx)
- Dual Outlet Power Adapter (http://amzn.to/1jJEnjx)
- Goo Gone Pen (http://amzn.to/1gVT1Uw)
- GPS (http://amzn.to/1omXqj7)
- USB Barcode Scanner (http://amzn.to/1m0mHNC)
- Wireless Barcode Scanner (http://amzn.to/1kvEzlj)
- Bestek 150W Inverter (http://amzn.to/1lHJ3lF)
- Brother QL-1050 Label Printer (http://amzn.to/1hfvhW3)
- 2-3/7" Thermal Label Roll (http://bit.ly/Rh2lpz)
- 4" Thermal Label Roll (http://bit.ly/1vQs3lv)
- Heat Gun (http://amzn.to/TB0X36) (Not essential, but greatly speeds up the removal of retail price stickers, and can also be used for ad-hoc shrink-wrapping)

I also have the wireless hot spot feature of my smartphone enabled. This feature allows your phone to act as a wireless router, which allows you to connect your laptop through it, providing Internet access anywhere you can get a wireless signal. Contact your wireless provider to enable this feature. It costs about $20 per month.

There really isn't much more to it than that. Unless you're at the ends of the earth, which probably wouldn't present many opportunities for Traveltage anyway, assuage any concerns knowing that you can buy anything you need. What a great business!

IN CLOSING

It's been fun sharing what I know about Traveltage with you. I hope you get value from it and that it helps you reach your goals. Now it's time to take action!

Viva la Traveltage!

Tim
Tim@Traveltage.com

P.S.: I want your feedback! Please leave a review here (http://amzn.to/1omXTSy). Thanks so much!

RECOMMENDED READING

Books are great (I'm quite a fan of them myself), but you must take action to be successful. No book can tell you everything you need to know – you learn best by experience. Now on to the reading list:

The 4-Hour Workweek: Escape 9-5, Live Anywhere, and Join the New Rich (Expanded and Updated) by Timothy Ferriss (http://amzn.to/1m0npu9)

This is the blueprint for lifestyle design. I have read it multiple times, and it always inspires me. Treat this as a potpourri of ideas you can implement to create the lifestyle you want. The ideas in this book DEMAND a paradigm shift in order to accomplish them. I've found it takes time and effort to test the ideas out, as well as to overcome past conditioning. Also, these ideas aren't widely practiced, or accepted in society. All this adds up to a need to be a non-conformist, if you hope to be successful with lifestyle design. It's not always easy, but it is tremendously rewarding and satisfying. For the most part, you will be swimming against the tide, and people will not understand what you're trying to accomplish. So be it.

Barcode Booty: How I found and sold $2 million of 'junk' on eBay and Amazon, And you can, too, using your phone by Steve Weber (http://amzn.to/1goIhxw)

My first exposure to the concept of Retail Arbitrage. I read this book in a single sitting, and implemented the strategies later that day. On my first scouting trip, with minimal effort and using only the Shopsavvy app (before I discovered more sophisticated apps like Profit Bandit) on my Android phone, I found items with low sales ranks that would net me 60%, after all expenses. I was blown away, considering other investments I was familiar with, and the effort needed to generate that type of return. Little did I know that this was just the beginning, and 60% isn't all that impressive! Steve is an experienced author and e-commerce expert who has a knack for distilling subjects down to the essentials. You can learn a lot from him. Highly recommended.

Make Thousands on Amazon in 10 Hours a Week! How I Turned $200 Into $40,000+ Gross Sales My First Year in Part-Time Online Sales! by Cynthia Stine (http://amzn.to/1oci2Nz)

Cynthia is a very thorough author. Her style is very straightforward and her guidance can get you up and running in no time. Additionally, she provides ongoing guidance via her blog, which is also highly recommended.

Arbitrage: The Authoritative Guide on how it Works, Why it Works, and how it Can Work for You by Chris Green (Formerly: *Retail Arbitrage: The Blueprint for Buying Retail Products to Resell Online*) (http://amzn.to/1oZfdiQ)

Chris Green is a master of Retail Arbitrage, and his book is the definitive work on the subject. After all the books I've read on investment and various others, I felt like I was spinning my wheels a lot of the time. All I needed to do was read this one for a comprehensive overview of the process. *Arbitrage* is a must-read.

Life Nomadic by Tynan (http://amzn.to/1k0NbMc)

Author Tynan makes some great points that will get you to rethink how you spend your time, and what you want to accomplish in your life. Couple his ideas with the Traveltage philosophy to see what's truly possible.

The Tiniest Mansion by Tynan (http://amzn.to/1kad69c)

Tynan's second book is devoted to full-time living in an RV. Most of this book pertains to a specific RV (the Rialta), and aftermarket modifications the author has made to make it more livable. He thinks outside the box and gives some general tips on RV living. His preferred model of RV, the Rialta, may not be practical for Traveltage due to space constraints, but his ideas could be easily applied to other RVs.

Getting Things Done: The Art of Stress-Free Productivity by David Allen (http://amzn.to/1jJFDDj)

This is a book with a huge following. There's a reason for that: it works. Do you find yourself constantly stressed, with too much to do? Are you not getting the results you want? Do you need to manage your time better? There are techniques in this book that will help.

As applied to your FBA business, it can help you stay on task, doing what you need to maximize your results, as efficiently as possible. Also, there are several apps available that follow the methods outlined in the book. The one I use is "DGTGTD," available free for Android devices. There are many similar apps available. Explore the Android/Apple marketplaces and do some experimenting to find the one that works best for you.

Blue Ocean Strategy: How to Create Uncontested Market Space and Make Competition Irrelevant by W. Chan Kim and Renee Mauborgne (http://amzn.to/Rh1s0f)

A study on how to succeed in competitive markets. There are case studies of such giants as Yellow Tail Vineyards, Southwest Airlines, and Cirque du Soleil, among others. These companies have found success in competitive markets simply by tweaking the traditional business model, so they stand out from the competition. In a nutshell, how do you compete? Find ways to differentiate, and you don't have to compete at all! Look for creative ways to apply these ideas to your FBA business. Can you bundle items together, making it likely that you're the only seller on Amazon?

The Long Tail: Why the Future of Business is Selling Less of More by Chris Anderson (http://amzn.to/1goJ7dL)

The "Long Tail" phenomenon explains how obscure products once relegated to dusty shelves remain in demand, even if they aren't exactly sought after by the masses. Because the Internet makes things readily available and findable, such items can be easily purchased by connoisseurs. This book will open your eyes to how commerce is transforming and how even the most unlikely items can still be profitable.

RESOURCES

That Kat! Radio (http://bit.ly/Rh9lCR)

Kat Simpson discusses all things e-commerce related. She frequently has prominent authors and product developers who provide information, services and products to help make your FBA (or eBay) business successful.

Also included at this site are the archives of FBARadio. This is no longer being produced, but the archives are worth listening to. The show featured an all-star cast of FBA experts (Chris Green, Bob Willey, Lisa Suttora, Kat Simpson).

Frequent guests such as Skip McGrath, and Cliff Ennico, among others, provided detailed information from sales strategies to legal and tax issues. While the information is no longer being updated, there is still a wealth of information to be learned by listening to the archives.

There are many interviews with interesting guests (including yours truly, and yes, I'd like to think I'm interesting), discussing all aspects of building your business with FBA.

Skip McGrath's Website (http://bit.ly/1goNtS7)

Skip provides a wealth of information on all things e-commerce related. His free newsletter is chock full of advice and resources to grow your business.

ScanPower (http://www.ScanPower.com)

ScanPower provides many services that can make you more efficient and make the task of preparing and shipping your inventory less of a chore.

FBA Forum (http://www.FBAForum.com)

This site is hosted by Bob Willey. Bob is mainly known for his expertise in books, but also shares a wealth of knowledge as a longtime eBay and FBA seller. Here you can interact with him and the FBA community.

Howazon.com & ThriftingForProfit.com (http://thriftingforprofit.com/)

Debra Conrad & Beth Sawicke's websites provide comprehensive information; a wide array of how-to videos, product reviews, FBA tips and tricks, podcasts and guides are available, many of them free. From beginner to advanced, there is something here for everyone.

Automate My Small Business (http://www.AutomateMySmallBusiness.com)

Excellent, free content for automating your small business. This is no longer being produced, but the archives are worth listening to. Matt Dotson and Brandon Kennington, the hosts of the show, follow the philosophies espoused by Tim Ferriss, and provide concrete examples of how to go about accomplishing them. If you're already using FBA, you have many of the principles they discuss already covered, but there is always more to learn. Highly recommended, and the price is right!

Lifehacker (http://www.LifeHacker.com)

Always interesting content on lifestyle design. You could read this site every day, and come away with enough information to reinvent yourself perpetually. Provided, of course, that you would want to do that.

EReaderIQ (http://www.EReaderIQ.com)

This site compiles a daily list of free Kindle books. The titles range from business to religion, and everything in between. There are usually several titles each day that appeal to me, and some have literally been life changing.

If you have a Kindle, great, but you don't need one, since you can read using the Kindle for PC, Kindle for iPhone, or Kindle for Android apps, all of which are free. You can't go wrong! But, there is one caveat: You need to act quickly. Most of the time, the books are only free for a limited time – usually 24 hours. The link remains active, but if you don't act quickly, you'll miss the opportunity to get it free.

Kindle Buffet (http://www.kindlebuffet.com)

Another site which compiles free Kindle book listings. The service is similar to EreaderIQ, but has more comprehensive reviews, as well as a daily email notifying you of all the free offerings. Like EreaderIQ, the books are available free for a limited time only.

FBA Step by Step (http://www.fbastepbystep.com/)

The blog of Cynthia Stine, author of *Make Thousands on Amazon in 10 Hours a Week!: How I Turned $200 Into $40,000+ Gross Sales My First Year in Part-Time Online Sales!* (http://amzn.to/1oci2Nz) Cynthia produces an informative free newsletter and blog. She is excellent at explaining timely issues affecting FBA sellers. Her archives are also a great reference.

Book to the Future (http://www.booktothefuture.com/)

The blog of Nathan Holmquist who is the author of *Selling on Amazon's FBA Program - Earn $2-5K Per Month Shipping Boxes of Books to Amazon* (http://amzn.to/1jcGuXd). He is a veteran in the industry. On his blog, he provides valuable tips to grow your business, as well as unique sourcing strategies in his free newsletter.

Traveltage (http://www.traveltage.com)

I couldn't very well write a book and leave my own site off the list, could I? Sign up to be notified of updates and additional information. Email me at Tim@Traveltage.com. I look forward to hearing from you. Maybe we'll cross paths, with smartphones in hand, and full carts of profitable merchandise, one day soon!

TRAVELTAGE PRODUCTS

Here is some additional information on some of the products I personally recommend and use:

Design Go Luggage Travel Trolley (http://amzn.to/1mcXrFr)

This is a favorite of mine. It's designed for carting luggage around, and because it's specifically designed for travel, it is amazingly lightweight, durable, and compact. I use it to move the myriad boxes of merchandise I'm shipping to FBA. It's affordable too; about $25 on Amazon.

It folds flat, and has an 18" footprint when collapsed. You can easily stow it in a carry-on bag. It's small enough to fit under the seat of your car, so you can use it at home in your business, as well as on the road.

You can use any manner of collapsible hand trucks available on the market, but most are not as lightweight and compact as this one.

American Weigh Scales Table Top Postal Scale (http://amzn.to/1niRmLo)

Since it runs on A/C power or AA batteries and is relatively lightweight and compact, this scale can be used at home and on the road as well. It is accurate and inexpensive (about $20 on Amazon). The readout can be customized to lbs, kg, and oz. It also has a "hold" button which is useful when a large box obscures the weight display.

American Weigh Scales LS-110 Digital Luggage Scale (http://amzn.to/1jczvgN)

This is the one I use on the road the most. It's reasonably priced at around $15 on Amazon, and it does the job well. It passes the compact and lightweight tests with flying colors, weighing only 5 oz. and having dimensions of 7" X 2". It is more than adequate to weigh anything you'll find to ship on the road.

Child-Safe Blunt-Nosed Scissors (http://amzn.to/1md32vq)

If you're trying to travel light, and still have what you need on the road, these are a godsend. One of the main benefits is that airport security doesn't have an issue with them. I have had no issues traveling through many security check-points in major airports with my blunt-nosed scissors in my carry-on luggage. Mine are shaped like a starfish! No doubt this tames the threat that they could be used for anything nefarious.

There are even some scissors that are made completely of nylon – no metal at all, but I can't vouch for their efficacy, and sadly, I don't think they're available in the form of any sea-dwelling creature.

TRAVELTAGE BONUSES

Go to Traveltage.com/bonus-downloads/ for these free bonuses:

1. PrinterShare Mobile Print walkthrough
2. Brother QL-1050 Printer setup

EVERYTHING YOU EVER WANTED TO KNOW ABOUT PROFIT BANDIT

Profit Bandit is packed with features. It is available for both Android and iOS. It gives you great market intelligence and can help you avoid making costly mistakes. Use this guide to understand how to get maximum benefit from it, and customize it. Courtesy of SellerEngine (http://bit.ly/1jBQQEB). Used with permission.

ANDROID GUIDE:

1. Activates camera for scanning.

2. Tap a specific sell price to update your Profit Calculation.

3. Highlighted offers are from Amazon.

4. Tap to adjust sell price based on item condition.

5. Tap these icons to view Add-on, History or item listing on Amazon

10. Manually enter a barcode or search terms.

9. Tap for special features (eBay, PriceGrabber, CamelCamelCamel, etc.) Note: You can also tap in large black space below.

8. Tap to be taken to Amazon to sell your item. You will be asked to sign in. Can also be used to add item to Buy List (adjust in Settings).

7. Tap to manually adjust your Buy Cost or Sell Price.

6. Your Profit. Tap to see the full calculation. Can be displayed in $ or % (adjusted in settings).

Adjust your item's Buy Cost/Sell Price or Condition.

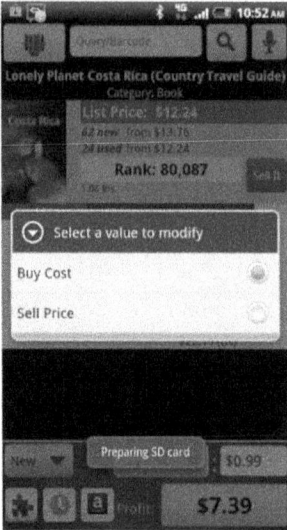

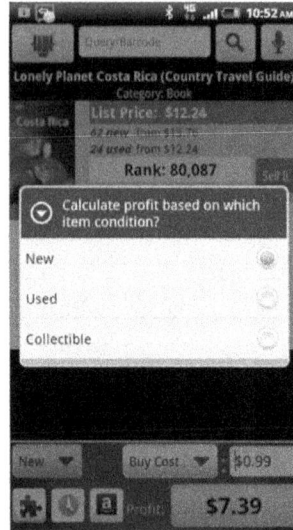

1. When manually searching be specific to limit the number of results.

2. The number after the pound sign (#) is Sales Rank.

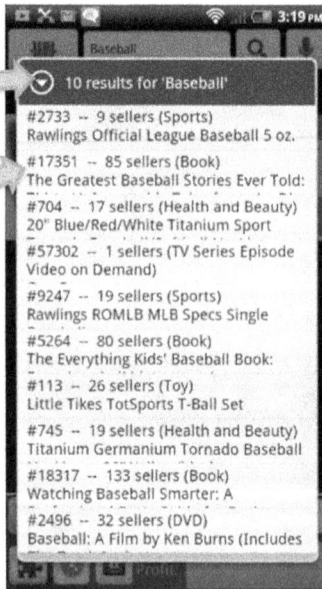

1. Profit Calculation Detail includes Selling Price, Shipping Credit, Buy Cost, Commission and VCF, and anything else that you adjust in Settings.

Note: Sell Price defaults to $.01 below the lowest price in the condition selected.

Profit Calculation Detail

+ $13.75 (Sell Price)
- $1.00 (FBA: Pick & Pack)
- $0.21 (Inbound Shipping)
- $0.74 (FBA Weight Fee)
- $0.01 (30-day Storage Fee)
- $2.06 (AZ Commission: 15%)
- $1.35 (Variable Closing Fee)
- $0.99 (Buy Cost)

PROFIT = $7.39

OK

New   Buy Cost $0.99

Profit $7.39

Lonely Planet Costa Rica (Country Travel Guide)
Category: Book

List Price: $12.24
62 new from $13.76
24 used from $12.24

Rank: 80,087

1.06 lbs.

FBA	62 New	24 Used
$12.24 (A)	$17.73	$15.69 (G)
$12.25 (A)	$17.74	$17.32 (VG)
$13.76	$17.94	$17.67 (VG)
	$18.81	$17.69 (VG)
	$20.13	$17.93 (LN)
	$20.97	$17.97 (LN)
		$19.92 (LN)
		$22.19 (LN)

1. Note: Tap the Settings button on phone to make this appear. Tap to add item to shipment.

2. Tap to email support or view FAQ.\.

Add to shipment   View shipment

Email Support   FAQ   Settings

4. Tap to view Shipment.

3. Tap to view Settings.

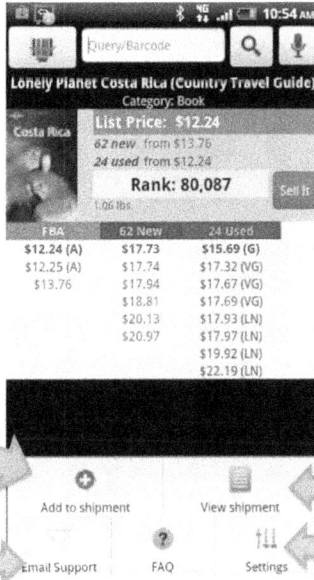

77

To add items to Shipment, first enter a Location/Supplier (optional) then enter the Quantity that you're purchasing. Item will then be added to your Shipment.

5. Tap to clear the contents of the Shipment.

1. Tap X to remove item from Shipment.

4. Tap to visit the Amazon listing page for an item in your Shipment.

2. Tap to save the Shipment as a CSV.
Note: Press phone's settings button to pull up this menu.

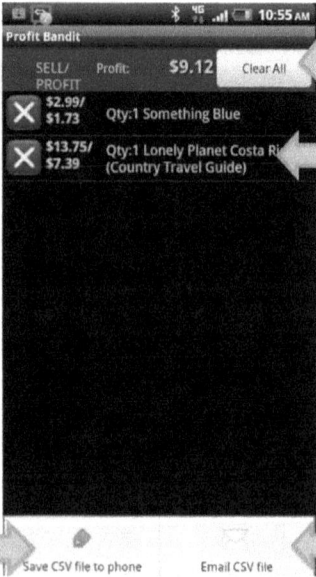

3. Tap to email the Shipment as a CSV file.

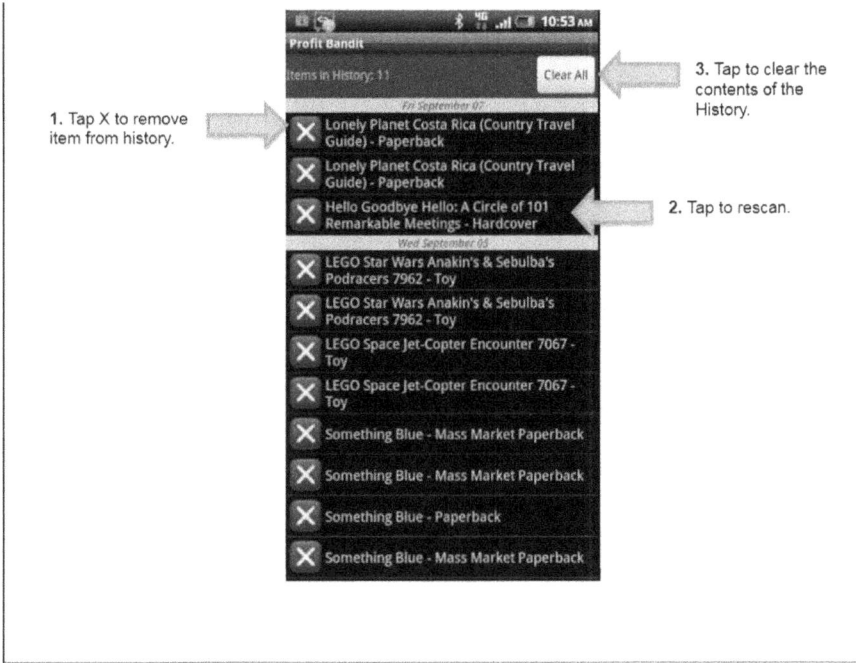

1. Tap X to remove item from history.

3. Tap to clear the contents of the History.

2. Tap to rescan.

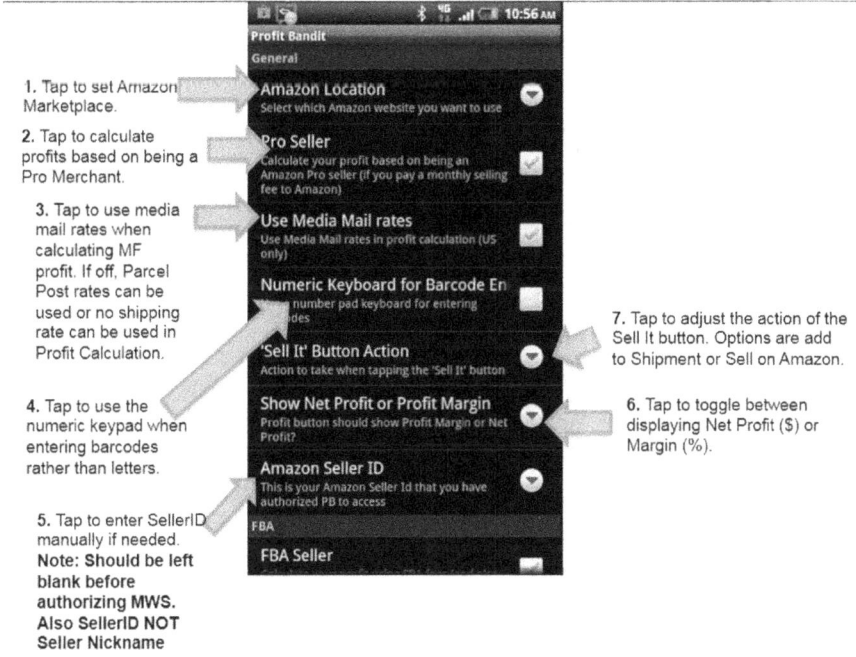

1. Tap to set Amazon Marketplace.

2. Tap to calculate profits based on being a Pro Merchant.

3. Tap to use media mail rates when calculating MF profit. If off, Parcel Post rates can be used or no shipping rate can be used in Profit Calculation.

4. Tap to use the numeric keypad when entering barcodes rather than letters.

5. Tap to enter SellerID manually if needed. Note: Should be left blank before authorizing MWS. Also SellerID NOT Seller Nickname

7. Tap to adjust the action of the Sell It button. Options are add to Shipment or Sell on Amazon.

6. Tap to toggle between displaying Net Profit ($) or Margin (%).

79

1. Tap to calculate profit using FBA fees.

2. Tap to set your FBA inbound shipping rates.

3. Tap to allow one-handed scanning by shaking the phone.

FBA

FBA Seller
Calculate your profit using FBA fees (and also show other FBA sellers)

FBA Inbound Shipping Rate
Average Shipping rate for sending items to Amazon distribution center (cents/lb)

Sell Price based on FBA
Calculate the projected sell price based on the lowest FBA offer (if available)

Seller Information

Show sellers
Download sellers for the item

Show sellers for every category
If turned off sellers will only be shown for the selected condition (and FBA if you're an FBA seller)

Special Functions

Shake to Scan
Turn this on to allow one-handed scanning by shaking the phone to start the barcode scanner

Continuous/Batch Scan

5. Tap to use the lowest FBA offer for default selling price. Can be overwritten by tapping any offer or manually entering a selling price.

4. Tap to show sellers for all conditions, not just your selected condition.

1. Tap to turn on Continuous/ Batch Scan Mode.

2. Tap to set alert based on profit threshold.

3. Tap to set alert based on Sales Rank threshold.

4. Tap to have Profit read aloud.

5. Tap to have Sales Rank read aloud.

6. Tap to have the number of sellers read aloud.

Special Functions

Shake to Scan
Turn this on to allow one-handed scanning by shaking the phone to start the barcode scanner

Continuous/Batch Scan
Allows you to scan many items at once for later access

Alerts

Profit Alert
The phone will vibrate when the profit is above the specified amount (set to very large number to disable)

SalesRank Alert
The phone will vibrate when the SalesRank is below the specified number (set to 0 to disable)

Speak Aloud

Speak profit amount
Reads the profit amount aloud using TTS

Speak SalesRank
Reads the SalesRank aloud using TTS

Speak Number of sellers

1. Tap to choose the app to use for scanning barcodes.

2. Tap to include FBA inbound shipping cost in profit calculation.

3. Tap to include FBA Storage fee in profit calculation.

4. Tap to include sales tax based on your buy price in profit calculation.

6. Tap to include postal rate in profit calculation.

5. Tap to include VCF in profit calculation.

Adjust Profit Bandit's display colors

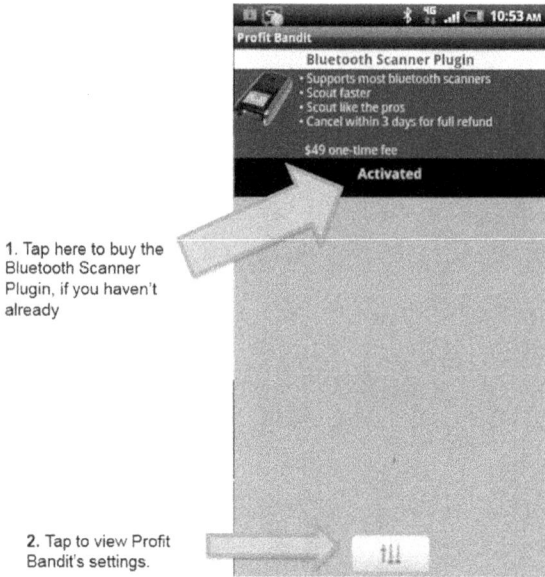

1. Tap here to buy the Bluetooth Scanner Plugin, if you haven't already

2. Tap to view Profit Bandit's settings.

Connecting a Scanfob

OPN 2002

- Pair with your phone
  - Go to your phone's bluetooth settings and discover the Scanfob
  - Hold down the small function key for about 5 seconds
  - Follow the on-screen instructions
  - Refer to the instructions that came with your Scanfob: http://bit.ly/opn2002
- Download and run SerialMagic Gears
  - Tap Connect
  - Hold down the small function key for about 5 seconds
  - That's it!
- Return to Profit Bandit and start scanning
  - Email support@profitbanditapp.com for more help

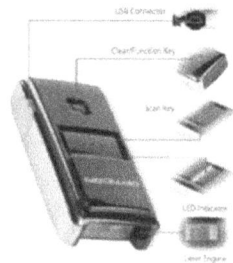

IPHONE GUIDE:

1. Activates camera for scanning.

2. Tap to view product image. **Note: Not that useful since we only have access to small images now.**

3. Tap a specific sell price to update your Profit Calculation (6).

4. Manually adjust your buy price (item cost or desired selling price).

5. Tap these icons to view Buy List, Bluetooth Add-on, Scan History, Settings (Left to Right)

11. Manually enter a barcode or search terms.

10. Tap for special features (eBay, PriceGrabber, CamelCamelCamel, etc.)

9. Tap to view the item's Amazon Product Page.

8. Tap to be taken to Amazon to sell your item. You will be asked to sign in. Can also be used to add item to Buy List with quantity and location (adjust in Settings).

7. Your Profit. Tap to see the full calculation. Can be displayed in $ or % (adjusted in settings).

6. Tap to adjust you sell price based on item condition

1. Merchant Fulfilled Profit Calculation includes Selling Price, Shipping Credit, Media Mail Rate (adjustable in Settings), commission and VCF. Can also include $.99 fixed listing fee.

Note: Sell Price defaults to $.01 below the lowest price in the condition selected.

MF Profit Calculation

+ $13.07 (Sell Price)
+ $3.99 (Shipping credit)
- $2.89 (Media Mail rate)
- $2.56 (AZ Commission: 15%)
- $1.35 (VCF)

PROFIT = $10.26

OK

1. FBA Profit Calculation includes Selling Price, Pick and Pack, Oversize (if applicable), inbound shipping (adjustable in Settings), commission and VCF.

Note: Sell Price defaults to $.01 below the lowest price in the condition selected.

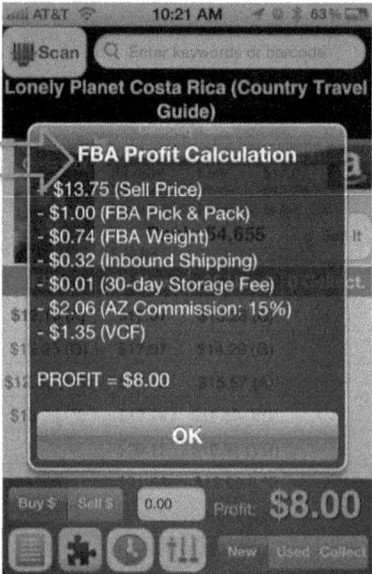

FBA Profit Calculation

- $13.75 (Sell Price)
- $1.00 (FBA Pick & Pack)
- $0.74 (FBA Weight)
- $0.32 (Inbound Shipping)
- $0.01 (30-day Storage Fee)
- $2.06 (AZ Commission: 15%)
- $1.35 (VCF)

PROFIT = $8.00

OK

Buy $ Sell $ 0.00   Profit: $8.00

New   Used   Collect.

---

1. Tap to return to scanning view

Back   Buy List

2. Tap to add the item currently on the scanning view to the Buy List.

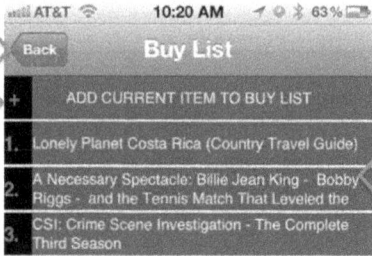

+ ADD CURRENT ITEM TO BUY LIST

1. Lonely Planet Costa Rica (Country Travel Guide)

2. A Necessary Spectacle: Billie Jean King - Bobby Riggs - and the Tennis Match That Leveled the

3. CSI: Crime Scene Investigation - The Complete Third Season

5. Tap to review the details of a particular item or to remove that item from the Buy List.

3. Email the Buy List as a CSV with columns for ASIN/UPC, Title, Author, Category, Condition, Buy Price.
Note: iPhone must have a mail account enabled.

Send as Email (CSV)   Clear All

4. Tap to clear the contents of the Buy List.

1. Tap to return to scanning view

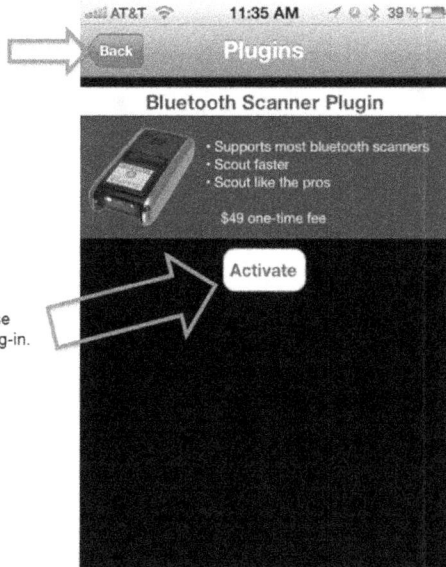

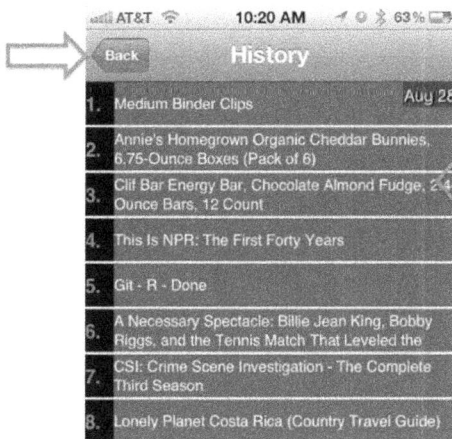

2. Tap to purchase the Bluetooth plug-in.

Bluetooth Scanner Plugin

- Supports most bluetooth scanners
- Scout faster
- Scout like the pros

$49 one-time fee

Activate

1. Tap to return to scanning view

5. Tap to review the details of a particular item in the History.

History

1. Medium Binder Clips — Aug 28
2. Annie's Homegrown Organic Cheddar Bunnies, 6.75-Ounce Boxes (Pack of 6)
3. Clif Bar Energy Bar, Chocolate Almond Fudge, 2.4-Ounce Bars, 12 Count
4. This Is NPR: The First Forty Years
5. Git - R - Done
6. A Necessary Spectacle: Billie Jean King, Bobby Riggs, and the Tennis Match That Leveled the
7. CSI: Crime Scene Investigation - The Complete Third Season
8. Lonely Planet Costa Rica (Country Travel Guide)

3. Email the History as a CSV with columns for ASIN/UPC, Title, Author, Category, Condition, Buy Price, Location and Quantity. **Note: iPhone must have a mail account enabled.**

Send as Email (CSV)

Clear All

4. Tap to clear the contents of the History.

Settings (General / FBA)

Status bar: AT&T · 11:34 AM · 39%

Back — **Settings**

General

1. Tap to return to scanning view

2. Tap to set Amazon Marketplace.

3. Tap to use media mail rates when calculating MF profit. If off, Parcel Post rates can be used or no shipping rate can be used in Profit Calculation.

4. Tap to include/exclude $.99 closing fee from Profit Calculation.

5. Tap to set to calculate profit as either FBA or MF seller.

Amazon Location: US | UK | Canada | France | Germany

Media Mail: On | Off   Pro Merchant: Yes | No   Scanner App Choice: ZBar | Pic2Shop

"Sell It Button Adds to Buy List"   OFF

Profit Display Type: Total Profit | Margin %

Amazon Seller Id [ ]

FBA

Seller Type: FBA | MFN   Sell Price based on FBA: Yes | No

Inbound Shipping Rate: 30 cents/lb

Seller Information

6. Tap to set your FBA inbound shipping costs.

7. Tap to use lowest FBA price for Selling Price.

8. Tap to enter SellerID manually if needed. **Note: Should be left blank before authorizing MWS.**

9. Tap to toggle between displaying Total Profit ($) or Margin (%).

10. Tap to use the Sell It button to add items to Buy List.

11. Tap to use Pic2Shop scanning app. You have to install this free app.

Settings (Seller Information / Alerts / Profit Calculation)

Status bar: AT&T · 11:34 AM · 39%

Back — **Settings**

1. Tap to return to scanning view

Seller Information

Show Sellers: Yes | No

Show Sellers for All Conditions? Yes | No

Special Functions

2. Tap to scan by shaking the iPhone

Shake To Scan: On | Off   Batch Scan Mode: OFF

Alerts

3. Set an alert for when a scanned item's Sales Rank is below a threshold

SalesRank Vibrate Alert: If under 5   Profit Vibrate Alert: If over 99.99

Profit Calculation

Sales Tax Percent: 0.00 %

FBA Inbound Shipping Cost: ON

FBA Storage Fee: ON

10. Tap to display selling prices.

9. Tap to show only sellers of your selected condition by default.

8. Toggle batch scanning mode. Batch scanning modes saves all scans to history for later review. Profit Calculations are not displayed for each scan.

7. Set an alert for when calculated profit exceeds a certain threshold.

6. Tap to include local sales tax to apply to your item cost.

5. Tap to include FBA inbound shipping in Profit Calculation.

4. Tap to include 30-day Amazon FBA storage fee in Profit Calculation.

1. Tap to return to scanning view

5. Tap to include postage in Profit Calculation. **Note: If Postage Rate is OFF, it will not show any Postage Rate, even if Media Mail is ON**

4. Tap to include VCF in Profit Calculation.

3. Tap to visit the Profit Bandit FAQ.

1. Tap to email support@profitbanditapp.com

SCOUTING TIPS - WHAT MAKES A GOOD OR BAD TRAVELTAGE PROSPECT?

Here are some examples of items I have scanned using Profit Bandit. Use these as general references to help you make better sourcing decisions.

Sales Rank: About as good as it gets!
Traveltage Logistics: Excellent
Verdict: Buy if margin is good enough

This item is perfect for Traveltage. It is compact and lightweight. There are only 72 items at the time of this scan that are more highly rated in the printing supplies category!

The brownish background in the FBA column indicates that Amazon themselves is selling this item. In general, competing with Amazon with all its market clout, is a bad idea. If you can get this item cheaply enough and still make a profit, this is an excellent prospect that will likely sell as soon as you ship it to Amazon. At a buy cost of $5, the net profit is just 84 cents – too thin for my tastes, but if I could get it for less, this would be a definite buy.

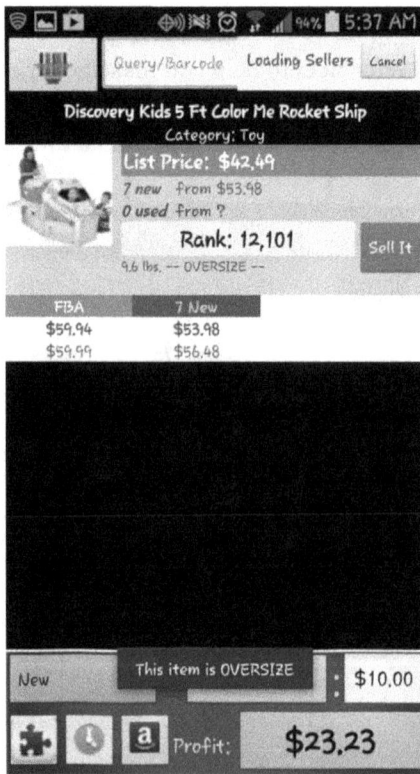

Sales Rank: Very Good
Traveltage Logistics: Poor
Verdict:Avoid

This item is oversize, so you will incur additional fees when the item sells, as well as more fees for storage until it does sell. Make sure you have enough margin to compensate for these fees, or avoid items like this entirely.

For Traveltage purposes I would avoid this item because of its size and the additional logistics involved with shipping. However, I might consider this at home because of the healthy margin. Making $23 for a $10 investment is a no-brainer!

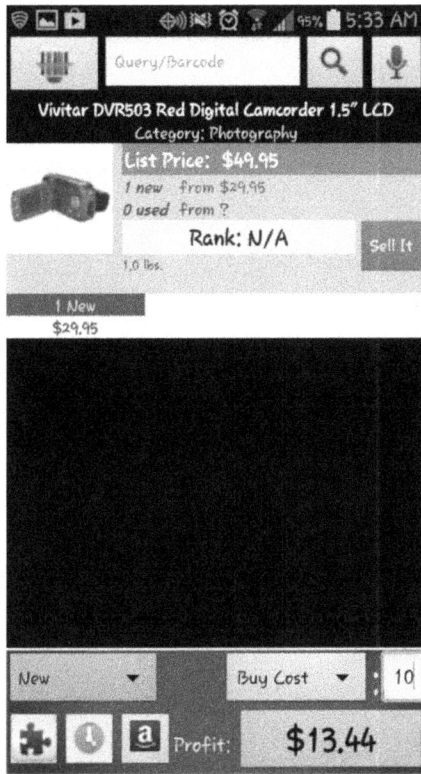

Sales Rank: Unknown
Traveltage Logistics: Very Good
Verdict: Avoid

Although this item is compact, lightweight, and appears to have a healthy margin, it is unattractive because there is no sales rank. Until the item actually sells, it's impossible to know if the current price will attract buyers. It's generally best to avoid items without sales ranks and focus on ones that do. If you just can't pass it up, tap the title or sales rank area to get an idea of its value using recent pricing data from CamelCamelCamel.com, eBay.com, Pricewatch.com, etc.